# Gunsmith Tools, Cutters & Gauges; a Primer

**Gunsmithing Student Handbook Series**

**#4**

Compiled and Edited by
Fred Zeglin

Contributors:
in alphabetical order:

Clymer Precision Inc.
1605 West Hamlin Rd, Rochester Hills, MI 48309

Dave Manson Precision Reamers
8200 Embury Road, Grand Blanc, MI 48439

JGS Precision Tool Manufacturing
60819 Selander Rd, Coos Bay, Oregon 97420

Pacific Tool and Gauge
675 Antelope Rd, White City, OR 97503

Sporting Arms and Ammunition Manufacturers' Institute, Inc.
11 Mile Hill Road, Newtown, Connecticut 06470

Copyright© 2019

ISBN: 978-0-9831598-6-5


Library of Congress Control Number: 2019920345

Published by
4D Reamer Rentals LTD.
432 E. Idaho St., Suite C420
Kalispell, MT 59901
www.4drentals.com

# FOREWORD

Fred Zeglin's excellent "Gunsmithing Student Handbooks" show why it's important to have both high-quality gunsmithing tools and expert knowledge. Success as a gunsmith is not possible if you have only one without the other.

Fred's newest book in the series, "Gunsmith Tools, Cutters and Gauges: A Primer" is a great source of knowledge about precision machining – a skillset critical to your advancement as a gunsmith. This book shows what tools you need and allows some of the best machinists out there to teach you how to use those tools, demonstrating the processes required to make world-class, tack-driving rifles and pistols.

This book delivers the same high-quality education as the other books in the series Fred has written so far on topics like understanding headspace, chambering precision rifles and both Ackley and wildcat cartridges.

Do yourself a favor, and get all of Fred's books, not just this one. It will be absolutely worth it.

**Pete Brownell**
**Brownells**

# Acknowledgments

Colonial Arms

Brownells Inc.

Gordy Gritters, Gordy's Precision

Todd Wilms, Clymer Mfg.

Dave Kiff, Pacific Tool & Gauge

David Manson, Dave Manson Precision Reamers

Kenny Humbert, JGS Precision

Dewain Q. Zeglin, Z-Hat Customs LLC

Sporting Arms and Ammunition Manufacturers' Institute, Inc.

# TABLE OF CONTENTS

# REAMERS FOR FIREARMS:

## What every gunsmith should know!

Many types of reamers are used on firearms. The primary differences are in what they are designed to accomplish, the technology is nearly identical to common reamers otherwise.

## Chamber Reamers

There are just a few makers of chamber reamers in the United States that specialize in this work. Boutique reamer makers come and go; there are of course makers in other countries. It's rare to see reamers from other countries so we will concentrate on American makers.

Most modern reamers have five (5) or six (6) cutting flutes. Five flute reamers are normally a special order item from the reamer makers and have become popular for barrels with 5R rifling. Rimfire or small caliber reamers may come with less flutes simply for the ease of manufacturing. The number or cutting flutes has zero (0) effect on the ability of the reamer to do its job, as proven by single flute reamers (cannon reamers as seen here).

**Figure 1 Cannon Reamer. One cutting edge.**

Multi-fluted tools, such as chamber reamers, tend to center themselves in the bore. Nevertheless, chamber reamers are piloted to insure that they do cut concentrically.

## All Chamber Reamers are Form Cutters

That means these reamers contain all the dimensions and features of the chamber they are designed for. So a standard chamber reamer always has the body, shoulder, neck and throat required for the cartridge to fit into the chamber and be fired. All modern chamber reamers will have a pilot, they are available with both fixed/solid pilots and removable/bushing pilots. Both styles are capable of producing accurate chambers. We will cover pilots later.

**What direction do I turn this thing?**

The reamer turns clockwise when cutting, or the barrel would turn counter clockwise on the reamer in a lathe. Running the tool backwards will damage it.

**What about belted or rimmed calibers?**

**Figure 2 Belted Magnum Chamber Reamer**

Belted or Rimmed reamers are exactly like the reamers described above, except they include the rim or belt cutting surfaces at the base of the reamer. Again, they contain all the features of the chamber in a single cutter.

**Roughing chamber reamers** as the name suggests, cut a large amount of material out to reach chamber dimensions, they are necessarily smaller in diameter than the finish reamer. So, you will need a Finisher chamber reamer to achieve the desired finished chamber dimensions. Roughers are most commonly used in production situations where time is a big factor. They save time when you are cutting many chambers for the same cartridge. Some small custom shops will use a resize die reamer as a rougher as a money saver.

**Finish chamber reamers** cut the chamber precisely to the cartridge dimensions. When retaining the same barrel bore, often a Finish reamer is all that is needed to chamber or re-chamber.

**Re-sizer chamber reamers** are for cutting a full length sizing die. If you are requesting a custom chamber reamer and expect to reload, it is recommended to order a re-sizer chamber reamer to have a matched set for precision loads.

## Reamer Nomenclature

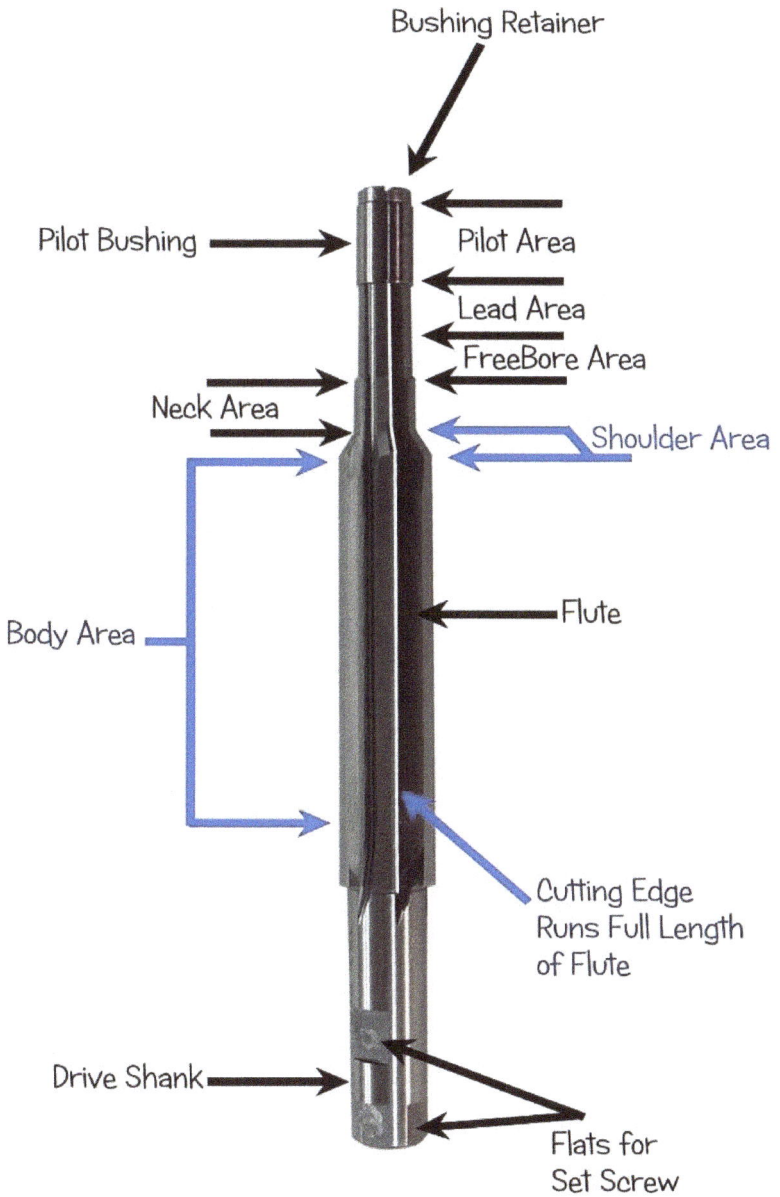

**Figure 3 Average Rimless Bottleneck Chamber Reamer**

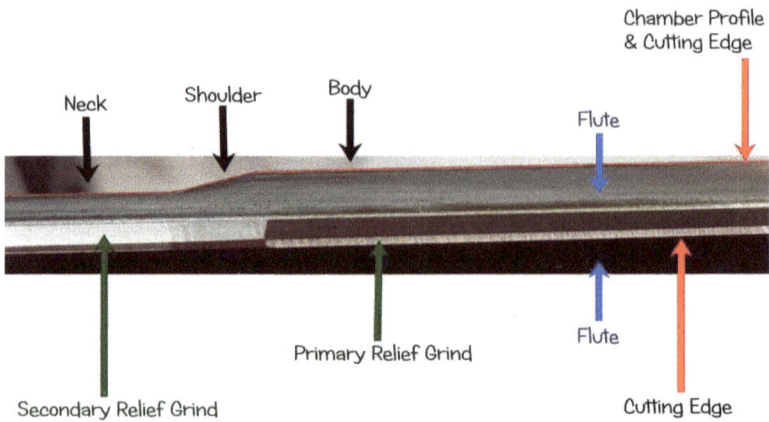

Figure 4 Nomenclature for Facets of the Reamer Flutes, Note the red along the cutting edge at the top of the picture, shows profile/form of reamer.

**Custom Reamers** These tools may or may not work with SAAMI standard ammunition depending on the dimensions specified by the customer. It is necessary to fully understand headspace and the relationship between ammo and the chamber when ordering custom tools.

Custom reamers can be ordered from reamer makers that have custom features or dimensions to the customer's desire. These are not standard reamers and may lack or include any feature the customer indicates.

For example, there are reamers with:

- No throat
- Zero Freebore
- Custom Freebore (short or long)
- Tight neck
- No-turn neck
- No Belt
- No Rim
- Tight dimensions (Match)
- Loose dimensions for semi-auto & full-auto reliability
- Custom dimensions (for your fantasies)

## Using Reamers

Feeds and Speeds are a common question. RPMs and feed rates below are based on a 30/06. Depending on the diameter of the tool, you may need to go faster or slower because it affects the surface speed of the reamer.

1) High speed steel (HSS) chamber reamers: 75-300 RPM, feed rate .004 to .006 per revolution.

2) Depth of a single cut with the throat, neck and shoulder engaged in the cutting process is about .050" because of chip load in the flutes, unless you have flush coolant from the muzzle.

3) Carbide chamber reamers: Begin at 200-400 RPM, feed rate .004 to .006 per revolution, for CNC applications, feed .050 to.200 per peck, assuming coolant flush from the muzzle. This will vary due to diameter and shoulder angle of the chambering reamer. The amount of chip build up will vary somewhere in this range. Also, coolant pressure and flow will vary the amount of feed per peck. There are many variables which may affect the outcome, a few include: coolant, oil, barrel steel, temperature of cutting fluids and the machines you are running.

4) Form tools such as center reamers, counter bores, muzzle crowns and breech counter bores: 30-70 RPM. Bore reamers: High speed and carbide 200-400 RPM; feed between 4" and 6" a minute.

*For use in a CNC machine you should check with the reamer maker for feeds and speeds.*

## Do I need to use a lubricant when reaming?

Absolutely. Use a quality cutting oil appropriate to the steel you are working with. Good cutting fluid will control heat by reducing friction, will prevent chip welding to the cutting surface, will increase tool life and improve surface finish of the workpiece.

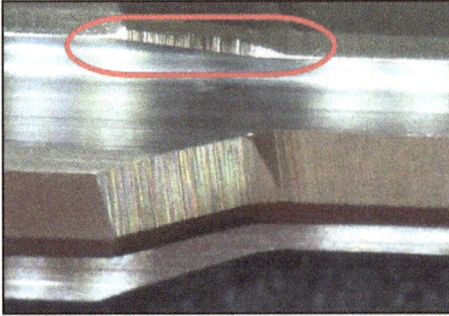

*The reamer shown here was allowed to run against something hard, most likely Chrome washed or Melonited bore, every flute was damaged.*

*Far left: This is the rim cutter on a reamer for a rimmed cartridge. Note that red lines indicate the original shape of the cutter.*

*Arrows on the right indicate both angles of the rim cutter are severely damaged. This tool was run against a hardened part, such as an extractor or ejector star of a revolver. Engage your brain…*

## Reamer Holder

It's highly recommended to run reamers with a Floating Reamer Holder in a conventional lathe.

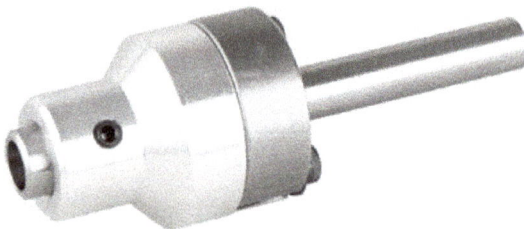

Floating reamer holders came into popular use because of the extreme difficulty in getting a bore lined up for zero runout. A slight error in concentricity will result in an oversize chamber by double the amount of the error. With the use of floating reamer holders, it is possible for the reamer pilot to follow an out of center hole and maintain correct alignment throughout the chambering process. Maximum correction should be no more than runout of .004" to .005". This creates a nearly perfect chamber and good finish.

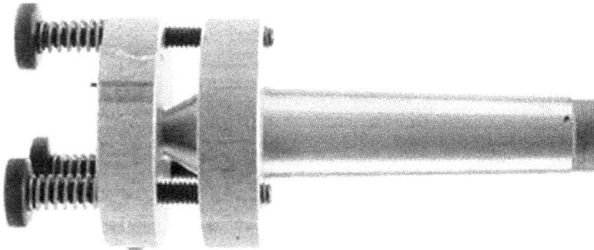

Even though a good lathe operator will have the tail stock dialed in as close to zero as possible, many machines will have misalignment of the tail stock in elevation. This is a major reason for using a floating reamer holder. There are many high quality floating reamer holders in the industry. A good holder will allow the reamer to float in all directions radially to the bore and allow for slight misalignment of the bore through the barrel blank.

Machinists who object to floating reamer holders are often accustomed to chucking reamers which only cut at the tip. Chamber reamers are cutting a long form and must follow a deep hole (the bore), this is a far different set up than many conventional machinists are used to working with.

As of this writing JGS has come up with a new floating reamer holder. Taking the lessons learned from their earlier designs and client feedback they designed a new tool that is more accurate and better aligned than the previous model. The new holder will be available with a variety of shank designs to suit the end user.

## Reamer Stops

Reamer stops are used to precisely set the depth of chamber cut on a lathe or mill. There are several designs out there, some are simple set screw collars that serve as a solid stop. Others provide micrometer adjustment to allow fine adjustment of the reamer stop.

## Can you force a reamer to cut off center?

Yes, so a good understanding of machine set up is necessary!

## Do You Need a Print for the Reamer?

*In most cases you do not.* Reamer makers today make reamers to SAAMI or C.I.P. specifications. The reason is simple, it reduces confusion and liability for all involved in the process. So you can simply use the standard prints from SAAMI and C.I.P.

The SAAMI web site is: https://saami.org

From the SAAMI Site: "As a part of our mission to provide standards for the firearms industry in the United States we freely publish the specification for SAAMI approved calibers." You can download all current information at no cost.

The Commission Internationale Permanente (C.I.P.) web site is: https://www.cip-bobp.org/en

C.I.P. like SAAMI publishes specifications on their web site.

When it comes to standard chambers if the cartridge and reamer is a standard design you can rely on the prints from these organizations. If you customize the design of the tool with different than standard dimensions then a print would be useful for your records.

Wildcat cartridges however are not registered with these agencies for standardization. That means the dimensions can vary widely. Even so, most of the reamer makers and wise wildcatters will follow the basics of design that are used by all the big factories. Why? Because there is no reason to reinvent the wheel.

## What is Chip Welding and Why Should You Care?

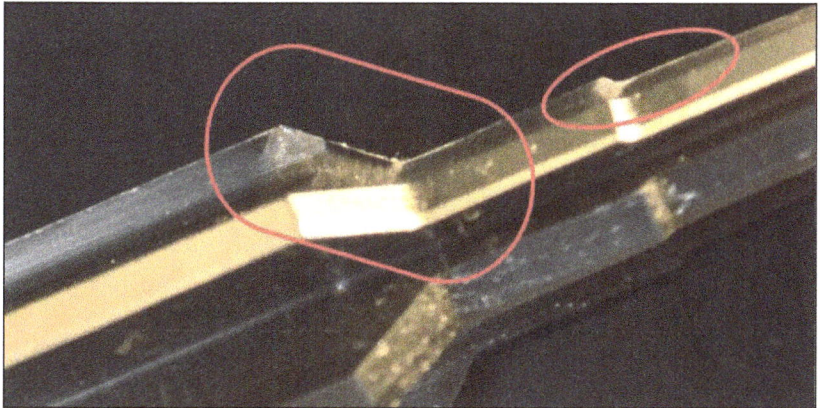

**Figure 5 Chip welded to the shoulder of this reamer.**

Chip welding is the result of several possible causes. It will reduce the ability of the reamer to cut a clean chamber. If allowed to build up too much it can cause a rough chamber finish or lead to groves in the chamber, normally at the shoulder.

1. Quality of the cutting oil, when proper cutting oil is used chip welding is greatly reduced, because the oil provides lubricity at the cutting edge needed for a clean cut.

2. Pushing the tool hard when cutting, i.e. high rpm, fast rate of feed or a combination of the two. Naturally, this ties back to the cutting oil too.

3. Quality or chemistry of barrel steel as well as the heat treat of the barrel can contribute to chip welding.

4. The diameter of the chamber, large diameter chambers with big shoulders are inordinately prone to chip welding.

5. Sharp shoulder chamber reamers like Gibbs and Ackley are more prone to chip welding. The shoulder on the reamer is doing the bulk of the cutting work. This area and the case mouth are the two places to watch for chip weld.

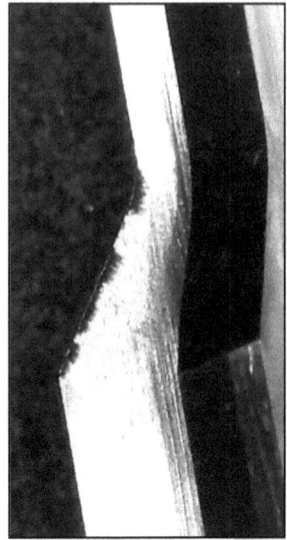

There are probably more, but these are the common and most likely causes.

## THE QUICK FIX...

Grab a piece of copper, an old penny will work, 1981 or older. The copper is soft enough that it will not damage the cutting edge of the reamer. The copper can be used to drag along the cutting edge where the build-up is. It will pop the chip off when it's thick enough. This will put the reamer back in service right away. It might take a little effort.

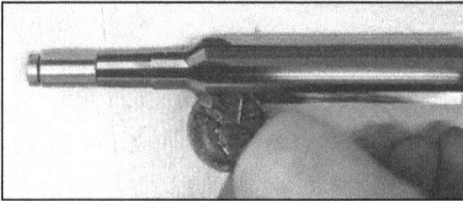

## HOW TO AVOID CHIP WELDING...

#1    Use a good quality cutting oil. It's getting harder to find these days but sulfur based cutting oils are the best. There are numerous products on the market that work fine. Spectrum cutting oil from Conoco, Brownells Do-Drill, Vipers Venom cutting oil, Rigid thread cutting oil and in a pinch even Tap Magic will work. This is not an exhaustive list, just a few you can usually find locally or on the Internet. See if you have a local oil distributor, call and ask what they have.

#2    Pushing the tool too hard, you can certainly control this one. Having it your way, right now, is great for fast food, not so much for machining custom firearms. Use plenty of cutting oil, slow down and put some precision and care into your work. Whether you are a hobbyist or a professional this advice will help you build guns that shoot circles around the competition. Your tools will last longer and they will produce a better finish in most cases.

#3    Large diameter chambers benefit from roughing of the chamber. This can be performed with roughing reamers (which are normally used for production work). Chambers can be roughed with a drill bit and boring bar as well. The boring bar is used to true up the chamber to the bore after drilling. This prevents the misalignment of the chamber to the bore. Since the reamer is not forced to cut as much material in a roughed chamber it is far less prone to metal build up.

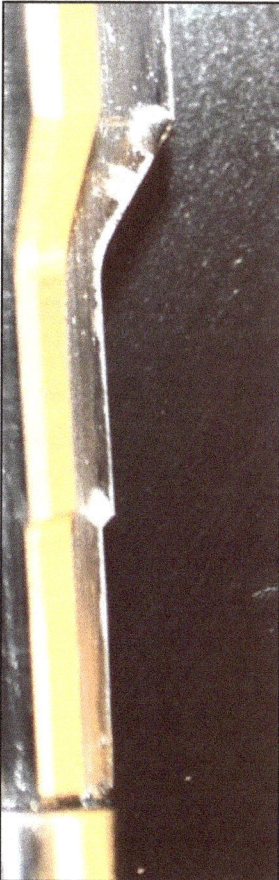

It is essential to understand that when roughing out a chamber you are putting added stress on the portion of the shoulder of the finish reamer that becomes the primary cutting point. Feeds, speeds and cutting fluid are extremely important in this case. You can easily damage or break the reamer because it is working on such a small area. Certainly, wear on the tool is increased.

#4    Barrel steel: It's certain that all the big name barrel makers use certified barrel steel. Even so from one lot to the next steel does vary. All you can really do is watch the tool and make sure it is not getting gummed up with chips welded to the cutting edge.

#5    Rough the chamber before using the finish reamer.  This saves wear on the finish reamer and saves a little time as well. Rougher reamers are nearly always used in production situations where many barrels of the same caliber will be chambered.

Once the chip weld starts it is a progressive build up.  Try the "Quick Fix" on page 17 before you try stoning.

Chip welding is of little consequence and can be easily cleaned off with a diamond lap or a stone by someone who understands how the tool works.

If you stone the outer periphery of the reamer you will ruin the tool in short order.  It will no longer cut the correct diameters.

**_Do Not_** stone the outer cutting edges of the reamer. Only stone on the inside of the flute, if you look at the geometry of the tool you will note that stoning there changes the tool a very tiny amount. When you stone the outside the dimensions are changed instantly and often far too much! If you are unsure, ship the reamer to the maker for cleaning.

## Misconceptions about Chamber Reamers:

*-This reamer seems way too long for the caliber I had in mind.*

The reamer makers produce reamer blanks in various lengths, they will choose the blank that is closest in length to the caliber the reamer is designed for.  So, in some cases the reamer will be longer than you expect, this has no effect on the finished length of the chamber.  You will use headspace gauges to set the proper chamber length.

*-If there is damage to any single flute of the reamer it will not cut a clean chamber.*

Not true.  So long as the damaged area is stoned out of contact with the bore the other flutes will cut just fine.

*-Feeds and speeds are fixed, variation from published numbers will never work.*

Not true. There are a huge number of variables that combine to produce the results you desire. Primary among them are the heat treat of the barrel, chemistry of the alloy, quality and limitations of your machine and the often overlooked quality of the cutting oil. Varying the RPM and the feed is the primary way to deal with these variables.

*-All flutes should cut evenly.*

Only if it's a single flute cutter. Part of the beauty of a multi-flute tool is that as it wears another flute can step in and take over the work. Most reamers will cut on several flutes, but it's not unusual if one or two carry a smaller chip load. The grinding wheel that cuts the reamer is wearing as the tool is cut. Very rarely do you see a "perfect" cutting tool.

*-Freebore is Magical.*

No, it's necessary, but cannot be used to revolutionize the firearms industry, otherwise that would have already happened long ago.

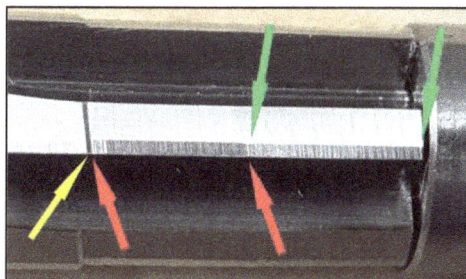

**Case Mouth marked Yellow.**

**Freebore is between the Red arrows.**

**The tapered leade is between the green arrows.**

**Pilot bushing is on the right.**

Modern chambers designed for jacketed bullets will normally have some freebore. This is to allow the bullet a place to reside in the barrel prior to firing so that the cartridge can be extracted from the chamber without leaving the bullet stuck in the rifling. It also allows the bullet to get started into the lands without causing an unsafe pressure spike when the cartridge is fired.

No amount of freebore, long or short, will produce magic results. P.O. Ackley, did extensive testing on freebore. He found that with as much as two inches of freebore there was no positive effect and little negative. We know that accuracy can suffer with excessive freebore. However, if the cylindrical freebore is kept to what we call bore rider dimensions today; accuracy remains extremely good because the bullet is held concentric to the bore of the barrel and is introduced to the rifling uniformly.

*-Freebore Length is Identical for Every Bullet.*

It is a static dimension in the chamber of your barrel.

However, when you try bullets with the same weight of varying designs or manufacture bullets will be seated at different lengths to achieve the same jump. Each bullet has a different shape from the groove diameter cylindrical section (contact surface) as it tapers down to the nose of the bullet. This tapered area, called the ogive, varies widely. So, when you try to seat a bullet to touch the lands, different bullets will have different seating depths.

For this reason reamer makers will offer reamers with any freebore you call out. But if you say, "I want .105" freebore for my 110 grain 6mm Schnickelfritz extreme B.C. bullet. Don't expect to have the same jump with a conventional hunting bullet, they are shaped differently. Reamer makers may have prints for popular bullets already drawn up.

Everything in life is a compromise, this is especially true for firearms. You can ask for any freebore length you desire, but it should be set to a nominal length that allows for a range of bullets unless you have a very specialized use. The length is far less critical than some folks would have you believe.

*-Zero Freebore*

This does not mean there is no throat at all. It means there is a leade cut on the rifling to allow for easy transition of a bullet to the rifling. Gunsmiths often order chamber reamers this way if they prefer to offer custom throat length for their customers. A separate throating reamer is required to set the custom throat length.

*-No Throat*

This means the reamer is ground smaller than the bore diameter ahead of the case mouth. Also used with custom throating.

*-CIP vs. American Throating*

C.I.P. is the European equivalent of SAAMI. European throats are a long continuous tapered area ahead of the case mouth. They do not have the parallel section for the bullet to rest in. This allows the bullet to engage the rifling "gently", causing less of a pressure spike.

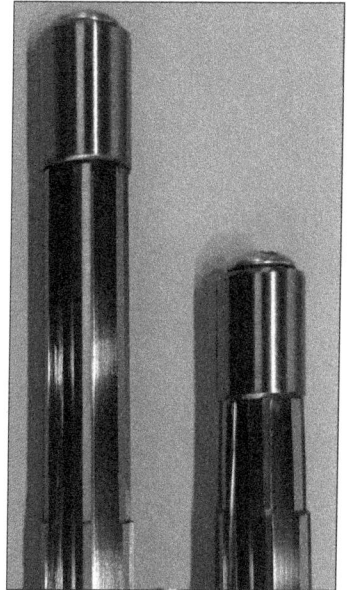

Accuracy is not hindered by the C.I.P. style throat. This type of throat is commonly found on European or C.I.P. calibers that do not have a SAAMI standard.

This simply represents two schools of thought that work equally as well in the real world.

***Neck Turning, uniforms the case's neck thickness, but it takes time and effort on every case.***

*-No Turn Neck*

Simply stating this when you order a reamer is meaningless. This normally refers to a tight neck reamer that is designed to work with factory ammo but allow less expansion on the neck. The concept is to seek greater accuracy without turning the necks on your brass and minimizing the working of the brass.

When ordering tools you would normally be asked to specify the diameter of neck you want. Be aware, brass varies from lot to lot and from one maker to the next. If brass is too tight in the neck of the chamber it will cause pressure spikes and can be dangerous.

Standard SAAMI type chamber reamers will normally have .004" larger diameter than the loaded ammunition as specified by SAAMI. A no-turn neck would normally be .002" over SAAMI ammunition. Often no turn neck dimensions would be found on "Match" reamers, unless some other dimension is specified by the client/gunsmith.

*-Reaming by hand*

It is possible and even common to finish a chamber with hand reaming the last few thousandths of an inch, setting the final headspace.

As a general practice however it is not advisable to try to hand ream an entire chamber. Can it be done? Probably, but the quality is not likely to be the best possible.

*-Match Reamers vs. "Match Grade"*

Historically, reamer makers have made reamers to the minimum SAAMI dimensions and designated them as Match reamers.

Today, Match dimensions can be for the entire chamber, or just for a few dimensions depending on the desires of the person ordering the tool. So in general Match reamers are those that are tighter than SAAMI standard but likely fall at the minimum SAAMI specifications.

Often the only dimensions that are called out are the neck diameter and the freebore length. This means some factory ammo may not fit in such chambers because ammunition could be made to maximum tolerances and still be within SAAMI specifications.

Since "Match" reamers normally refers to reamers that are made to tighter dimensions than standard factory chambers, these closer dimensions mean the brass is closer to the chamber walls and is less disrupted when fired than in a standard SAAMI chamber. Tight dimensions are used in the search for accuracy.

Tight dimension chamber reamers will require special reloading dies be made to similar tolerances, otherwise any advantage is pretty well negated.

"Match Grade" reamers. Many makers will state that the quality of their tools is Match grade. This refers to the fact that they hold uniform tolerances and finish. All American chamber reamer makers are producing "Match Grade" tools today or they will be out of business.

*-Reamer Life*

Any chamber reamer, when treated well, used properly, kept clean and rust free will last a surprisingly long time. High Speed tool steel (HSS) used in chamber reamers is hard and tough. The makeup of barrel steel and how hard you push the reamer as well as the quality of the cutting fluid used will determine in large part how long tools last.

Many reamer makers place a date of manufacture on their tools. This is not a freshness date. Sometimes standard dimensions are changed over time, so it simply allows you to know when your reamer was manufactured. *A professional who cares for his tools can easily get 50 to 75 chambers* without any noticeable wear to the tool.

On the other hand, overloading the reamer with chips, feeding too fast, little or no cutting fluid, poor quality lube, tossing them in a drawer without protection and general misuse can kill a good tool in just one or two chambers. Treat reamers like the precision tools that they are and they will produce good chambers for years to come.

*-Chatter is always a result of a bad or dull tool.*

**False.** Chatter is caused by many factors. The technician can almost always solve the problem.

First among these is the fit of the pilot to the bore of the barrel. When the pilot is too loose it will allow the reamer to move around and gouge the barrel, thus - chatter. Correct pilot fit is .0005" to .001" smaller than the "bore" diameter of the specific barrel ("bore" refers to the dimension across the lands of the rifling, this is best measured with pin gauges).

RPM is the next culprit, often slowing down the RPM will stop chatter. Most of the reamer makers state that HSS reamers can run as fast as 250 to 350 RPM, this means you can try running up the spindle speed to stop chatter. Remember as you increase speed the feed must increase to balance the chip load.

Things like the heat treat of the barrel and/or the specific alloy can contribute to chatter. A reamer that worked beautifully in one blank may not like the next one. If you see the reamer is flexing under load, then you are feeding it too fast for that particular barrel.

Chambers with greater taper generally are more troublesome, in terms of chatter potential than chambers that are fairly straight-- cutting 300 Win Mag doesn't give the problems that cutting 300 H&H does. More taper translates into more feed pressure being required to cut a similar depth—this makes it difficult to feed the reamer at the proper rate and means there are no hard and fast speed/feed parameters.

Chambers with large differentials between neck and shoulder diameters also cause problems—cutting a 300 RUM chamber will likely be more problematic than one for a 308 Win. It should be noted here that some of the trouble experienced by 'smiths chambering calibers with large neck/shoulder diameter differentials is the result of their allowing the flutes to fill with chips.

Don't let flutes pack with chips to the point that the chips have nowhere to go. Besides producing a poor finish, this condition can cause the reamer to break, typically at the neck/shoulder junction. Clear chips before the flutes are filled; a 45-70 reamer can be run in much further before chip clearing than a 300 Win Mag. Watch the amount of chips in the flutes and clear accordingly.

When discussing the causes and cures of chatter, it's essential to realize, that chamber reamers are difficult cutting tools to use. Unlike a chucking reamer, which cuts only on its leading edge and produces a round hole of a certain size, a chambering reamer cuts along most of its length and produces a tapered hole.

If you do barrel work, you will experience chatter, more than once. It's almost never the reamer. Remember it's a poor workman who blames his tools. Check your set-up, change feeds and/or speeds, double check the fit of your pilot to the bore.

-*"This reamer chatters…"*

See discussion of chatter on previous pages. Unless you have dealt with the discussion of details about the causes of chatter then you cannot and should not blame the tool.

**Cures for Chatter:**

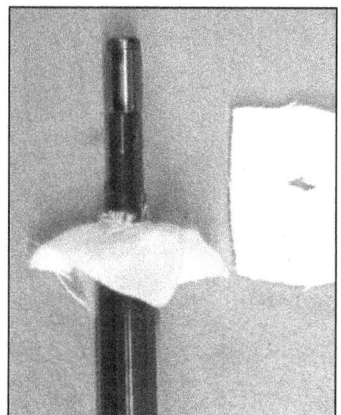

Cut a small slit in the center of a cleaning patch so the pilot can slip through it. Use good cutting oil. Allow the patch to feed into the chamber on the reamer. The cloth will dampen chatter. It may require many clearances of chips and new patches to remove chatter once it starts. Use a new patch with every cut.

Wax Paper works extremely well to dampen chatter and get a reamer cutting well. Tear strips of wax paper about ½ to ¾" wide, long enough to wrap around your reamer several times. Use good cutting oil. Feed the reamer wrapped with wax paper into the chamber. Always have it over the shoulder, or if no shoulder, up to the end of the case area on the reamer. You will need to use new wax paper every time you clear the chips.

With either method be sure to clear the reamer, clean the chamber and make sure no chips are allowed to remain. This prevents scoring the chamber with trapped chips. Lowering the RPM with either method is beneficial in cleaning up chatter.

Old Timers used a reamer loaded with Beeswax or heavy axle grease to accomplish the same thing. The only problem with these methods is the mess that ensues. Patches and/or wax paper are far easier to use and leave less of a mess.

Once the chatter is stopped, (often within .200" of full depth) you can normally stop using the dampening method and just use cutting oil to finish the chamber.

Do not let chatter get away from you. Stop what you are doing and solve the problem right away, minimize the damage and insure that you will save the barrel by being proactive.

# Pilots and Their Diameter are Critical!

As mentioned in the section on chatter a few pages earlier, pilot diameter is the most important factor *you* control in preventing or stopping chatter in a chamber.

Solid pilot reamers are traditionally made with a pilot diameter that is at the minimum expected diameter for barrels made in the U.S.

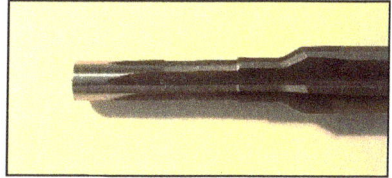

The idea is simple, by going to minimum specification the pilots will fit most any barrel you may find. It's not unusual for a solid pilot to be a few thousandths of an inch smaller than the bore (the diameter inside the lands of the barrel is the bore diameter). In short, making them as universal as possible.

Some guys will claim they cannot be accurate, that simply proves they have a lack of experience, on the contrary, they can be very accurate, producing chambers that win matches. But that is a separate subject.

So why do removable pilot reamers exist?

Because some folks like to remove every alibi they can from the process of chambering a barrel. Removable pilots allow you to utilize a pilot bushing that closely fits the bore of your barrel. This eliminates unnecessary run-out between the pilot and the bore of the barrel which might allow the chamber to be out of alignment with the bore.

No matter what size or type of pilot you are using, *it must slip* inside the bore. A slip fit on a pilot is normally .0005″ to .001″

29

smaller than the bore. Pilots that are too small (loose) for the bore allow movement of the reamer and therefore can promote chatter.

If the pilot is too large it will not slip in the bore. There are several bad outcomes possible from a pilot that fits too tightly in the bore:

- Damage to the lands ahead of the throat of the chamber caused by the friction of a solid pilot rubbing on the lands.

- Solid pilot and/or reamer broken, due to the stress of being too tight in the bore.

- Removable pilot too tight in the bore can cause the pilot to be forced back onto the reamer. Since there is no cutting angle where the bushing meets the flutes of the reamer this will impede the advancement of the reamer in the bore.

- Removable pilot too tight in the bore often causes the bushing to stick in the bore. If a gunsmith is paying attention and notices the tight bushing this will never happen.

- Air gauged match grade barrels are normally defined as those that have less than .0002" to .0003" (depending on the maker) variation in bore diameter from end to end. So if you try to stay too close to bore diameter with the pilot bushing you may start out with a slip fit but hit a bind a little way into the bore, especially if the barrel is not match grade.

- Removable pilot bushings that fit too tight can introduce enough stress to occasionally cause a reamer to break or chip.

Reamers for calibers smaller than 8mm seem to be more susceptible to the variables that cause accuracy problems. So pilot diameter and fit to the bore is much more critical with smaller calibers.

When you are talking about calibers that are 8mm and up (Big Bores) chambers are less prone to accuracy problems. Likely because the increased mass of the heavier projectiles in larger caliber simply overcome much of what causes issues in small calibers with light bullets. In short, you will learn that larger calibers are much less prone to accuracy problems.

Below are some pilot bushings that show damage because they were too tight for the bore. Truth is truth, SIZE MATTERS.

*Reamer pushed so hard that it cut the pilot.*

*Reamer pushed so hard that it swaged out the end of the pilot.*

*Bushing forced onto the reamer so that the throat started cutting to pilot.*

# In a nut shell: *If it doesn't fit, don't force it!*

# COMMON REAMER TYPES

### What is a "Barrel" Reamer?

A chamber reamer marked (B) or Barrel is designed for reaming in a barrel as opposed to the cylinder of a revolver.

So conversely, reamer marked (C) or Cylinder is not designed for use in a barrel. Why? These markings are used on calibers that are used in revolvers, thus cylinder. Because cylinders require a larger pilot diameter as the cylinder throat is normally about .001" larger diameter than the groove diameter for the specified caliber.

If a barrel reamer has a removable pilot, it can be used in a cylinder by changing the pilot to the correct diameter for the cylinder throat. These are sometimes called convertible reamers.

### Cylinder Throating Reamers

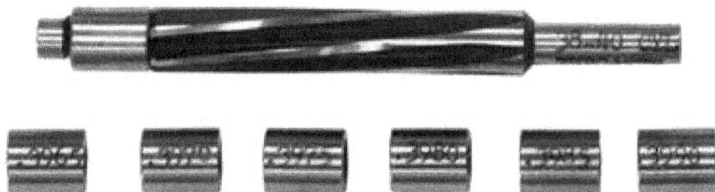

These are specialty tools used to ream the throat of cylinders for revolvers so that all the chambers have the same throat diameter. Manufacturing processes at big factories can produce cylinder throats that vary considerably in diameter from one chamber to the next. This causes accuracy issues in revolvers.

### Throating Reamers

Like chamber reamers all throating reamers have pilots built in. Throating reamers are designed to only cut the throat and lead in the barrel. American or SAAMI style throats normally have a

32

cylindrical section (with no taper) that provides a place for the protruding projectile to rest in the barrel ahead of the chamber for a short distance. The diameter of this part of the throat is normally .0005" larger than the specified bullet diameter. It will also include lead, that is, an area of taper cut on the rifling to allow the bullet to transition smoothly into the rifling with minimal disruption and pressure spike.

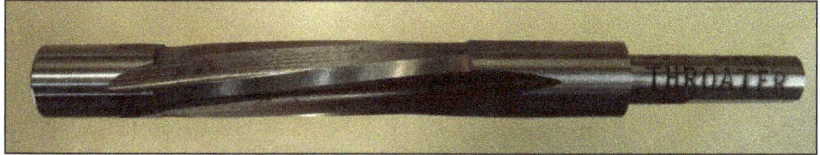

CIP style throats are common to European chamber dimensions. These throats are long tapered sections that do not include the cylindrical section found in American chamber designs. The idea is to allow the bullet to gently enter the rifling and minimize any increase in pressure that is caused when the bullet engages the rifling.

There are a few styles of reamers for throating.
- Straight Flute
- Spiral Flute
- Universal Adjustable

Spiral fluted reamers of any type are slightly better at avoiding chatter. When using throating reamers by hand it is very important to make sure the reamer does not slip in between the lands of the rifling, causing the reamer to engage far too much material at one time. This can break the reamer or damage the barrel or both.

The Universal adjustable style reamer has a stop that allows the user to set the depth of the cut.

**Neck Reamers**

A neck reamer is just like if sounds, a reamer that is designed to cut only the neck dimension of the chamber. Yes, they are piloted too. They serve a couple of purposes. Wildcatters may use them to create a "necked up" version of an existing cartridge.

Say you had a 25 caliber chamber reamer and you wanted to make a 30 caliber version of that cartridge. You can use a 30 caliber pilot on the chamber reamer to cut the body of the chamber and set the headspace. You could then use a 30 caliber neck reamer to complete the neck. Of course you would still need to throat the barrel.

Another use for neck reamers is to correct a chamber. Occasionally a client tries a "match" or "tight" neck chamber and finds they do not like the restrictions it places on the ammo they can use. A standard dimension neck reamer can be used to open the neck up to the standard diameter or length.

**Neck and Throat Reamers**

These reamers combine the neck and throat cutting dimensions in a single reamer. They can be custom dimensions or standard. All have pilots just like the other chamber reamers. They serve the same basic purposes as the neck reamers above.

Neck and throat reamers are commonly used for wildcat chambers because the gunsmith can have one reamer with the smallest neck and throat and use it as a body reamer for larger bore diameters. They can also be used to create long or short neck versions of cartridges.

*Neck and throat reamer.*

**Resize Reamer**

Reloading dies are cut with reamers made for that purpose. A Resize reamer is smaller in dimensions than the chamber and seldom has a throat area as this is not needed in a die. Resize reamers are often marked "RZ".

# Shotgun Tools

## Carbide vs. High Speed Steel (HSS)

Many shotgun bores, in particular inexpensive European bores are chrome washed. This makes the long lasting and easy to clean, but when it comes to modifying the bore it requires the use of carbide tooling. HSS tools will be damaged by chrome washed bores.

## Chamber Reamers

Shotgun reamers are very similar to other chamber reamers. The primary difference is that they are much larger in diameter and length than most chamber reamers. This added size means they have very large cutting surfaces.

Increased cutting surface requires more pressure to push the tool into the barrel to cut a chamber than with smaller chambers. These are not tools to be used by hand in most cases.

Just like the smaller chamber reamers we have discussed they have all the same features. They can be had in solid or removable pilot. Spiral flute or straight flute reamers are available, spiral flutes are less prone to chatter. Standard shotgun chamber tools include a rim cutter.

## Long Forcing Cone Reamers

These reamers have no rim cutter by design. Their sole purpose is to cut the forcing cone at the front of the chamber to a longer taper. This has a few effects. First, it lowers felt recoil. Second, it reduces the initial pressure spike when the cartridge is fired. Third, it reduces the amount of deformation of the shot as it is forced into the bore of the shotgun, which is assumed to improve shot patterns at all normal shotgun ranges.

Many factories will cancel your warranty when long forcing cones are cut. It is imperative especially on thin barreled guns that you measure to be sure a weak spot is not created by the longer forcing cone. It is up to the gunsmith to determine if the job is safe on a case by case basis.

Some modern shotguns have their barrels hard-chrome plated in the chamber and bore. High Speed Steel forcing cone reamers won't cut through this plating and attempting to do so may damage the tool. Check for the presence of chrome using cold blue: if it takes on the chamber area, the steel and can be cut; if the surface won't blue, it's likely chrome-plated and should be avoided.

Position the barrel(s) horizontally in a padded bench vise with the muzzles tipped slightly down. Clamp a suitable tap wrench on the shank square, cover the reamer with good-quality cutting oil and carefully insert it in the chamber, being careful not to scrape the sides. It's a good idea to place catch pans under the muzzle and breech ends of the barrel to catch any oil drips.

Turn the Long Forcing Cone reamer in a clockwise direction while applying firm forward pressure. The reason we recommend positioning the barrel(s) horizontally is that it's easier to apply necessary cutting pressure in this attitude.

With that in mind, take 10 or so turns with the reamer, then withdraw, clean both reamer and barrel and examine the area you just cut. The surface should not show any chatter marks (spiral lines/ridges), but should be fairly smooth. Continue the reaming process, stopping periodically to clean chips from the reamer and workpiece and to inspect your progress. Don't allow chips to build up to the point that they fill the flutes—this can cause chatter or a rough surface finish.

Long Forcing Cone Reamers are designed so that the body of the reamer is ground to the same taper and size as a standard shotgun chamber and will cut only if great pressure is applied. The leading section of the tool, however, cuts more rapidly, and blends into the body of the tool at chamber diameter. This means that the reamer will cut fairly easily until the body of the tool fills the chamber, when cutting effort will increase greatly. At this point also, the new forcing cone will blend into the existing chamber.

Generally, the finish left by these reamers is not bright and shiny, because of the long tapered cut. A cylinder hone is used to polish the new forcing cone. Flex hones are sometimes used for this purpose as well. Reamers are available for all gauges of shotgun bores.

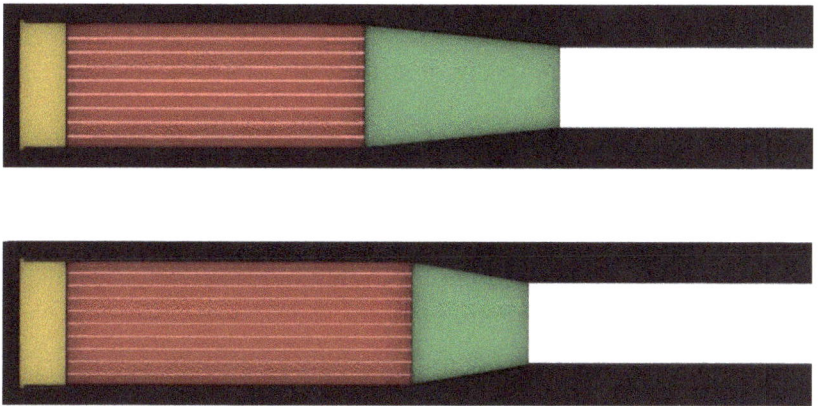

*Above are two shotgun chambers. On the left side of the image we have cartridges loaded in the chambers, the bore on the right. The green area ahead of the cartridge is the forcing cone, the bottom barrel represents a standard factory forcing cone. The top is a long forcing cone (LFC) after the barrel has been reamed out.*

**What does the word *Choke* mean when referring to shotguns?**

Strictly speaking, "choke" is the amount of difference in diameter between the cylinder portion of the barrel and the constriction at the end of the barrel. This determines pattern density of the shot charge. This difference is measured in thousandths of an inch. For instance, a 12 Ga. "Modified" choke will show a 0.020" difference in diameter. "Full" choke will show a 0.040" difference in diameter.

Different manufacturers, and even the same manufacturer over a period of years, may use different diameters in the cylinder portion of their barrel. There is no absolute standard to which all barrel manufacturers adhere to. That's why you will sometimes get a "tighter" or "looser" pattern from a given choke tube in a particular shotgun. Also, the brand, loading, and size of the shot will make a difference in many shotguns.

Two, otherwise identical shotguns from the same manufacturer may have very different preferences in ammunition. Finding the optimum pattern density may take some experimenting.

As a general rule, steel shot will pattern about one choke "tighter" than lead shot. Therefore, some choke tubes will say something like "Lead-Modified/Steel-Full" if they are made for steel shot.

Always check to be sure that your shotgun barrel and/or choke tubes are steel shot compatible before shooting steel shot in your shotgun. If in doubt, contact the manufacturer of your barrel, shotgun or choke tube.

Common fixed types of chokes:

Many factory shotguns come with a fixed choke barrel (part of the barrel). This means the muzzle is thicker than the main portion of the bore. The added thickness is inside the bore creating a tapered restriction. This is the conventional type of fixed choke on modern guns.

*Conventional*→

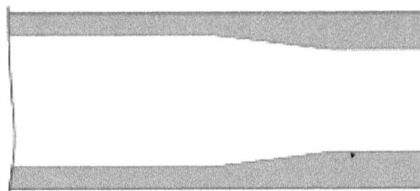

### Swaged Choke

This is sometimes found on old, very inexpensive single barrel shotguns. The end of the barrel was forged or swaged to a smaller diameter to form some degree of constriction at the muzzle. This could be done by heating the barrel muzzle red hot and driving it into a tapered hole. This type of choke has long since been discarded by modern manufacturers.

*Swaged→*

### Jug Choke

This is a type of choke that can be used to restore some degree of constriction to barrels that are cylinder bore, have been cut off behind the choke, or have no choke for some reason. One inch behind the muzzle, the barrel is bored or polished to expand the internal diameter. This oversized section can vary from two to three inches in length and be up to .040" over bore size.

**Jug Choke**

Shotgun bores vary widely by maker. For instance European shotgun bores are often as much as .005" smaller that American made shotgun barrels. American makers have varied the bore diameter for any given gauge by as much as .015" over the decades.

Why so much variation? Simple Shotguns are not a precision tool. However, choke diameters are pretty well set and can be relied upon for results. This works because a choke is a constriction at the end of the barrel, so as long as the constriction is the correct differential in diameter the result is predictable.

For each choke listed in the chart the amount of constriction is listed in thousandths of an inch.

| Shotgun Bore & Choke Basic Dimensions | | | | | | |
|---|---|---|---|---|---|---|
| **Gauge** | **10** | **12** | **16** | **20** | **28** | **.410** |
| **Average Bore Diameter** | .779 | .729 | .667 | .617 | .550 | .410 |
| Cylinder Bore | .000 | .000 | .000 | .000 | .000 | .000 |
| Skeet I | .005 | .005 | .004 | .004 | .003 | .002 |
| Improved Cylinder | .010 | .009 | .007 | .006 | .005 | .004 |
| Skeet II | .015 | .012 | .010 | .009 | .007 | .006 |
| Modiefied | .020 | .019 | .015 | .014 | .012 | .008 |
| Improved Modified | .025 | .025 | .020 | .019 | .016 | .011 |
| Full | .035 | .035 | .028 | .025 | .022 | .015 |
| Extra Full | .040 | .040 | .035 | .027 | .024 | .021 |
| Turkey | .045 | .045 | | | | |

## Colonial Arms Tooling suggestions for installation

| | | Minimum | Maximum |
|---|---|---|---|
| Gauge | Thread Size | O.D. | I.D. |
| 10 GA | .865x44 | .900 | .781 (True Size) |
| 12 GA | .812x32 | .845 | .736 (Rem Choke) |
| 12 GA | .812x32 | .845 | .736 (Win Choke) |
| 12 GA | .812x32 | .845 | .736 (Invector) |
| 12 GA | .795x44 | .825 | .736 (True Size) |
| 12 GA | .774x44 | .805 | .730 (Thin Wall) |
| 16 GA | .718x44 | .750 | .668 (True Size) |
| 20 GA | .675x44 | .700 | .626 (True Size) |
| 28 GA | .613x44 | .645 | .560 (True Size) |
| .410 | .478x44 | .510 | .416 (True Size) |

**Removable Choke Tools**

As with shotgun chamber reamers, these tools have a huge surface area and take more pressure to cut than their smaller cousins. This work is best done in a lathe. There are many patterns of choke tubes that are popular. A few are commonly available to the gunsmith:

- Rem Choke (Remington)
- Win Choke (Winchester)
- Tru-Choke
- Tru-Choke Thinwall

Most common removable choke tools are 12 and 20 Gauge. They are designed to be used as a set, a reamer, Tap and several pilot bushings. Other choke pattern/brand tools can be purchased, the procedures are essentially the same no matter the brand name.

*The reamer and tap above are used in conjunction with bushings that match the bore of the barrel to ream the correct steps for the screw choke, then the tap is used to thread the barrel, using the same bushing to align the tools.*

Its not unusual for a novice to think these tools are dull *even when new.* Below is a picture of a partially reamed barrel to show the quality of cut you should expect to get. The reamer is best used under power and it has a lot of material to remove.

*Notice the two steps in the barrel. The deeper step is what will become the seat for the choke tube (90 degree cut). The second, nearest the muzzle is the angled start for the threads.*

*This test cut was done with a reamer the client thought was dull. It is only deep enough to test the cutting edges of the two shoulders. This cut gives us a nice view of the shoulders and the finish.*

## Measuring For Screw-In Chokes

Before machining to accept screw-in chokes, you must measure the outside diameter (O.D.) to determine if there will be sufficient wall thickness after machining. "Mike" the O.D. of the barrel and the O.D. of the tap for the particular gauge. Subtract the O.D. of the tap from that of the barrel, divide by 2, and this will give the wall thickness after machine, **providing the O.D. of the barrel is concentric with the inside diameter (I.D.).** A sample calculation appears below.

*Barrel O.D. (12 Gauge)*     *.850"*
*Tap O.D. (12 Gauge) Win-Choke*™    *-.814"*
                                       *.036" / 2 = .018" Wall Thickness*

**It is not advisable to install chokes in barrels where the resultant wall thickness will be less than .015", providing the I.D. of the barrel is concentric with the O.D. If the I.D. is** <u>not</u> **concentric with the O.D., you will have to make your own decision as to whether the installation will be safe.**

You **CANNOT** install screw-in chokes in barrels whose inside diameter (I.D.) exceed the following dimensions     : **10 ga. - .780", 12 ga. - .735"; 12 ga. Thinwall - .728"; 16 ga. - .666"; 20 ga. - .624".** Exceeding these dimensions **WILL CAUSE DAMAGED CHOKE TUBES** and there is a **GREAT POSSIBILITY OF CAUSING A BARREL BLOW-OUT!** Check EVERY installation before firing to make sure the tube does not protrude into the bore. Back-bored or jug-choked barrels are usually not suitable for screw-in choke installation.

For a shotgun barrel to be machined successfully to accept 12 Ga WinChoke tubes, the barrel must measure at least .845" outside diameter (.815" cutting dia. Plus 2x the min. wall thickness). This figure assumes that the outside is perfectly concentric with the inside – most often NOT the case. Because of this, YOU will have to use your judgment concerning the safety of a particular installation.

Any pre-existing fixed choke or external choke device (like a Poly-Choke®) will have to be removed prior to any machining for screw in chokes. Cutting the barrel shorter will certainly allow you to remove existing chokes. It is also easy to ream out fixed chokes. This is commonly done using expandable reamers designed to open a hole a few thousandths of an inch at a time. Start with the tool set so it will cut about .004" to .010". Continue making passes with the expandable reamer until you are at cylinder bore +.000" -.001". Then you will be ready to use the screw choke reamer.

*Adjustable/Expandable reamer.*

If after measuring, installing WinChoke tubes seems questionable, consider a TruChoke or TruChoke Thinwall installation. If the barrel seems too thin for any of these systems, it's probably best to turn down the job.

Assuming installation can be done safely and you have the necessary tooling, machining of the barrel is done in the following steps:

(1): MAKE SURE THE GUN IS UNLOADED

(2) **Remove any existing choke
(ream out the fixed choke or cut barrel shorter to remove the fixed choke)**

(3) Ream the barrel for the desired choke tube system.

(4) Tap the threads in the reamed barrel with a tap designed for that choke pattern.

(5) Clean and deburr

Make sure you do not leave any chips, or dirt from the installation process in the threads just cut in the barrel.

## Choke Lube

Choke tube lube is essentially an anti-seize compound. It fills in the tiny gaps between the outside of the choke tube and the inside of the shotgun barrel, in the thread area, to keep the tube from getting ironed into the threads of the barrel. Also, by filling this area with lube, powder residue build up is virtually eliminated.

Powder residue build up is another reason that choke tubes can sometimes get stuck in a barrel after extended use. It is important to remove and clean the tubes as well as the tube seat in the shotgun barrel on a regular basis. Using choke tube lube will help eliminate any potential problems in this area.

Many shooters also use their choke tube wrench to occasionally break loose the tube by unscrewing it a quarter of a turn or so, and then re-tightening the tube to make sure it is properly installed on the tube seat. This prevents the tubes from accidentally backing out and causing damage to the tube and the end of the shotgun barrel.

# WHAT ARE HEADSPACE GAUGES?

Headspace gauges as produced by the firearms industry are actually a chamber depth gauge, in that they tell the technician/gunsmith how deep to cut the chamber.

Headspace gauges are designed to insure that the depth of the chamber will match the tolerances set forth by The Sporting Arms and Ammunition Manufacturers Institute, Inc. (SAAMI) for chambers and ammunition.

According to SAAMI, "In the interest of safety and interchangeability in the cartridge-firearm relationship, dimensional limits are reflected in the dimensions and tolerances shown on the cartridge and chamber drawings. Gauges, commonly referred to as headspace gauges, are utilized to measure dimensional characteristics of the firearm chamber."

**Defining Headspace:**

*Headspace in the firearm is the measured distance between the breech end of the gauge when fully seated against the datum point of the chamber and the breech face of the firearm when fully locked up in the firing position.* **Headspace is literally the space between the head of the cartridge and the breech face.**

Heaspace is the distance between the bolt face and case head.

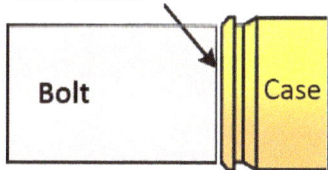

Critical things to understand about measuring headspace:

1. The proper use of Headspace Gages is the most reliable way to test the length of a firearm chamber.

2. Loose or excessive headspace (a measurable distance between the case head and breech face) is an impairment to accuracy and often is the source of poor groups.

45

Excessive headspace may lead to gas leakage around the case, partial or complete case head separation and in rare cases the sudden release of high pressure gas.

In most situations a crack in the case will develop or a case head separation will take place. There is only <u>one</u> <u>cause</u> of case head separations; it is <u>always</u> excessive headspace, whether in the gun/ammunition or both.

3. Insufficient or abnormally tight headspace will cause malfunctions, such as failure to lock/close. It is frequently diagnosed as a feeding issue by shooters. If the gun fires in this condition, it often makes extraction difficult and may cause dangerous stresses on the mechanism, which may, in turn, shorten component life expectancy or lead to failure.

**Choosing the Correct Gauge**

Some shooters are under the misconception that headspace is fixed over the life of the firearm. Headspace can increase after repeated use of ammunition that causes too much pressure. One should routinely check rifle chamber headspace every thousand rounds. If chamber headspace is excessive, the gun should be taken out of service until it has been inspected and repaired by a competent gunsmith.

Headspace Gauges are used to determine if a firearm's headspace is within acceptable limits. Headspace gauges can be made to any dimension, but are generally made to the industry-standard (SAAMI) minimum [Go] and maximum dimension [Field]. Tool makers offer an intermediate gauge known in the industry as the No-Go Gauge.

Headspace is measured differently, depending on whether the firearm's caliber uses rimmed, belted, or rimless cartridges. Gauges should be manufactured from top-quality, hardened steel and precision ground to American National Standards Institute (ANSI) and SAAMI tolerances. The Gauges are designed to provide an easy way to test for proper clearance between the head of the cartridge and the breech face.

1. **GO gauge:** Corresponds to the minimum chamber dimensions. If a rifle closes on a GO gauge, the chamber will accept ammunition that is made to SAAMI maximum specifications. The GO gage is essential for checking a newly-reamed chamber in order to ensure a tight, accurate, and safe chamber that will accept SAAMI maximum ammo.

2. **NO-GO gauge:** Corresponds to the maximum headspace recommend for gunsmiths' chambering new bolt-action rifles. This is *not* a SAAMI-maximum measurement. If a rifle closes on a NO-GO gauge, it may still be within SAAMI specifications, or it may have excessive headspace. To determine if there is excessive headspace, the chamber should then be checked with a FIELD gauge. The NO-GO gauge is a valuable tool for gunsmiths' reaming new chambers, in order to ensure tight and accurate headspace.

3. **FIELD gauge:** Corresponds to the longest safe headspace. If a rifle closes on a FIELD gauge, its chamber is dangerously close to, or longer than, SAAMI-specified maximum chamber length. This would indicate chamber headspace is excessive, the gun should be taken out of service until it has been inspected and repaired by a competent gunsmith. FIELD gauges are slightly shorter than the SAAMI maximum in order to give the tiniest of safety margins.

You will note on the Headspace Gauge prints from SAAMI that follow, only a "Minimum" and "Maximum" headspace dimension is given. Minimum corresponds to the Go gauge, Maximum to the Field gauge. The No-Go is what the industry sees as safe and reasonable maximum headspace for a newly chambered firearm. Most custom gunsmiths will hold much tighter tolerances in order to provide best accuracy and longevity of the guns they work on.

When checking headspace, ideally the bolt or slide should be stripped of anything that could cause a false reading (extractor, ejector plunger). Practically speaking, this isn't always possible. Needless to say, these checks must be done on an UNLOADED gun, with a clean chamber and bolt, in order to get a correct reading from the gauges.

One exception: In revolvers the "GO" gauge must rotate past the recoil shield; the "NO GO" and "FIELD" gauges should not. A feeler gauge can be used with the Go gauge to make sure exactly what the headspace is. Align the Go gauge with the firing position and run the feeler gauge in between the gauge and the recoil shield (breech face).

*NOTE:* It should go without saying; the chamber, bolt face and gauges must all be clean to give you a correct headspace measurement.

Chips and or oil in the chamber from reaming the work will give false readings. So will dirt or brass residue on the gauges or bolt face. While you're cleaning, make sure the locking surfaces of the bolt and lug recesses are clean as well!

**Headspace Gauges are precision tools. Treat them as such.**

Keep them free from abrasives, store them safely so they do not bump into other tools, protect them from rust and corrosion and keep them clean.

# How do you know what gauge to use for any specific cartridge?

Starting on Page 57 there is an interchangeability list. For headspace gauges. If you are unsure, check with a reamer maker to see what gauges are correct for your cartridge?

In case you have not discovered this yet, there are "Families of Cartridges".

I.E. 30-06 gauges work with all cartridges with the same case body and shoulder angle. Interchangeable with 30-06: 22-06,

6mm-06, 25-06 Remington, 270 Winchester 7mm-06, 8mm-06, 338-06, 35 Whelen and 375 Whelen.

There are many "Families". Look at the interchangeability list and you will spot them quickly.

. GAUGES FOR SHOULDER-BREECHING CARTRIDGES

FIGURE I
SHOULDER-BREECHING CENTERFIRE RIFLE HEADSPACE GAUGES

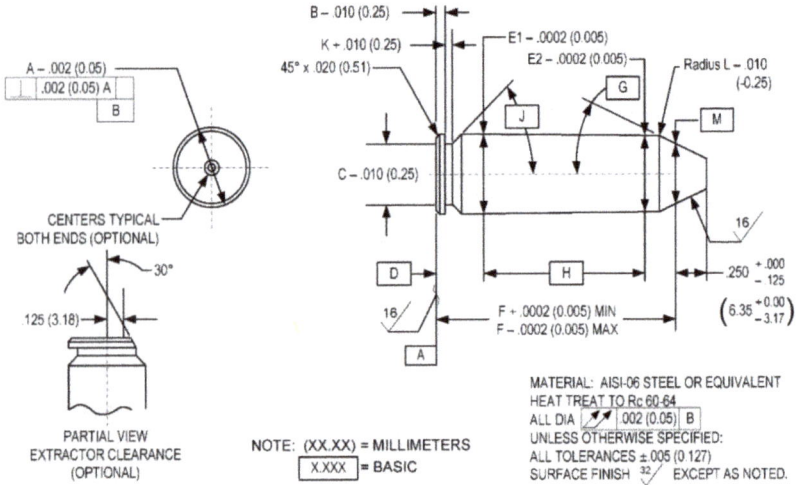

## Rimless Cartridge

In the print above, the distance between the bolt face (D) and a datum line (M) [determined by SAAMI] where the front of the cartridge rests on its shoulder when the bolt is closed equals correct chamber depth. Note that these gauges follow the general form of the cartridge body.

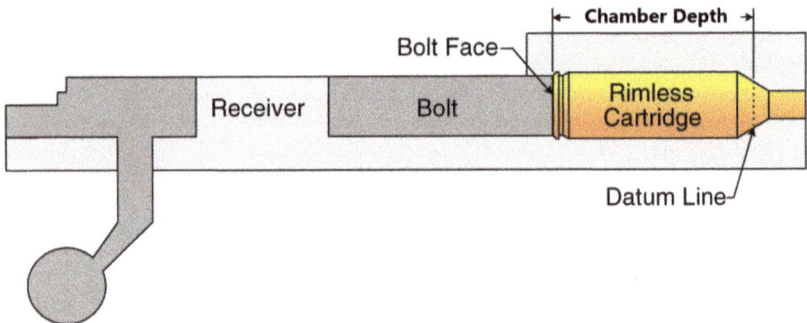

## III. GAUGES FOR RIM-BREECHING CARTRIDGES

**FIGURE III**
**RIM-BREECHING CENTERFIRE RIFLE HEADSPACE GAUGES**

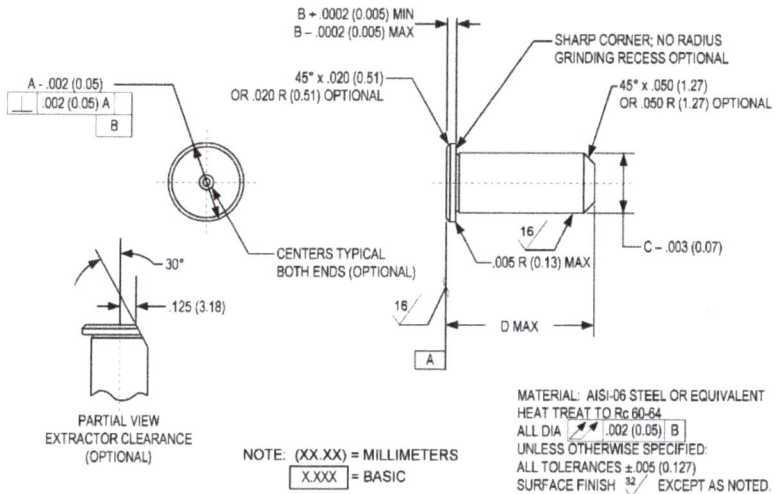

B + .0002 (0.005) MIN
B – .0002 (0.005) MAX

SHARP CORNER; NO RADIUS
GRINDING RECESS OPTIONAL

45° x .020 (0.51)
OR .020 R (0.51) OPTIONAL

45° x .050 (1.27)
OR .050 R (1.27) OPTIONAL

A – .002 (0.05)
.002 (0.05) A
B

CENTERS TYPICAL
BOTH ENDS (OPTIONAL)

C – .003 (0.07)

.005 R (0.13) MAX

30°

.125 (3.18)

D MAX

PARTIAL VIEW
EXTRACTOR CLEARANCE
(OPTIONAL)

NOTE: (XX.XX) = MILLIMETERS
X.XXX = BASIC

MATERIAL: AISI-06 STEEL OR EQUIVALENT
HEAT TREAT TO Rc 60-64
ALL DIA .002 (0.05) B
UNLESS OTHERWISE SPECIFIED:
ALL TOLERANCES ±.005 (0.127)
SURFACE FINISH 32 EXCEPT AS NOTED.

## Rimmed Cartridge

In the print above, distance between the bolt face (A) and the top/front of the rim (B) [chamber face on the breech of the barrel] when the bolt is closed. Note that these gauges are seldom the same shape as the chamber body as the rim is all that matters for dimensions. Gauges have been supplied by some makers as a coin only, since only the rim determines headspace.

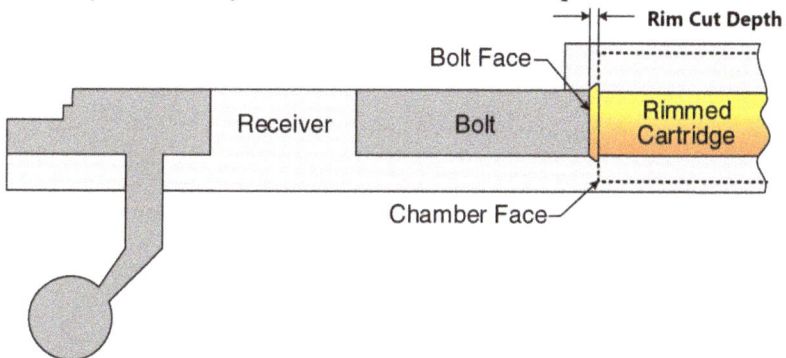

Rim Cut Depth

Bolt Face

Receiver     Bolt     Rimmed Cartridge

Chamber Face

## II. GAUGES FOR BELT-BREECHING CARTRIDGES

### FIGURE II
### BELT-BREECHING CENTERFIRE RIFLE HEADSPACE GAUGES

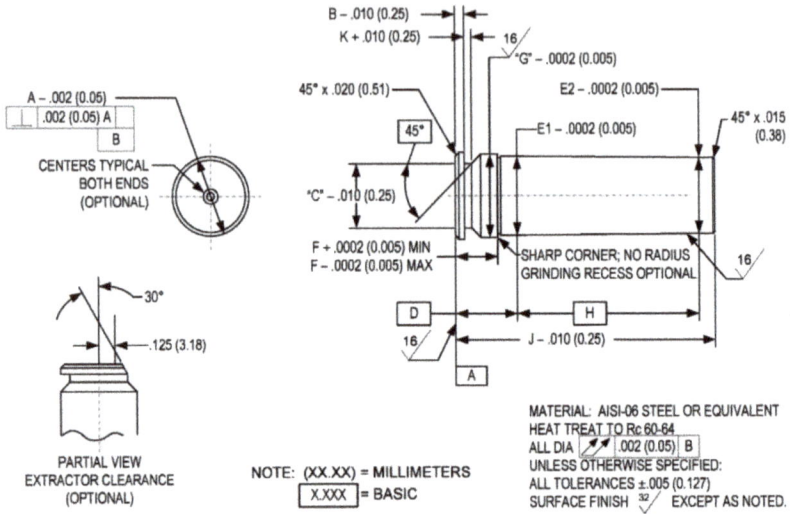

## Belted Cartridge

In the print above, distance between the bolt face (A) and the top of the belt (F) when the bolt is closed. Note that these gauges do not follow the form of the chamber, as the belt diameter and length are the only dimensions that matter.

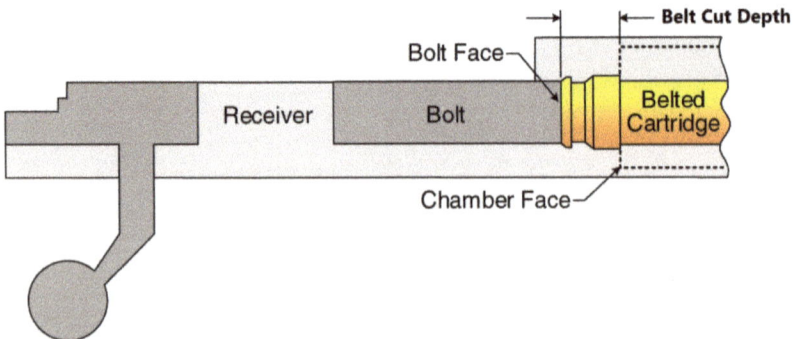

## How are "Improved" Chambers Headspaced?

The famed gunsmith, P.O. Ackley is the undisputed king of "Improved" cartridge designs, they are modified versions of standard calibers and have been popular for decades. Today, when an improved cartridge is designed it follows Mr. Ackley's rules for headspace, as published in his books.

Headspacing improved versions of rimmed or belted cases presents little difficulty and no need for special gauges, because headspace is controlled by the rim or belt—in the same manner a standard chamber would be headspaced.

Setting correct headspace of improved rimless chambers (Ackley or otherwise) is more involved because the cartridge is not held by the same contact points as in a standard chamber. Further complicating the headspace issue is the requirement of being able to safely fire a factory round in an improved chamber, with the result being a properly fire formed improved case.

When fire forming a standard cartridge in an improved chamber, the base of the cartridge contacts the breech face in the usual manner, but the front of the case is contacted only at the neck/shoulder junction and not along the entire length of the shoulder, see below.

Because the cartridge must be held securely against the breech face during fire forming, the dimension between the breech face and the neck/shoulder junction becomes critical. P.O. Ackley, recommended that this dimension be reduced by .004"/.006" from the standard minimum for a particular caliber. Reducing this dimension compensates for cartridge tolerances and ensures that fire forming can be done safely.

To chamber and existing barrel to an improved version of their original (factory) chambering must have their barrels set back by <u>at least</u> .004"/.006" to allow for safe fire forming of brass. Gauging the improved chamber is done per normal practice, with the exception that a lighter touch should be used. Ackley recommended that headspace gauges having the same shoulder angle as the original, but .004"/.006" *shorter* than minimum be used to headspace improved chambers.

This means that the gauge will contact only the neck/shoulder junction and breech face. An Ackley Improved "GO" gage is .004"/.006" shorter than standard GO gauge, and has the same shoulder angle. The standard GO gauge for the parent cartridge should be used as a "NO GO" in an improved chamber.

Failure to set the barrel back for bottleneck rimless cases will result in a cartridge that will not follow proper headspace rules for improved cartridge design. It is definitely not an Ackley and can be unsafe to fire.

Gauges made according to Ackley's guidelines may be used to headspace any caliber based upon the original case. For instance, 30-06 Improved gauges made Ackley style may be used to headspace all '06-based chambers from    22-06 Imp. through 35 Whelen Imp., or larger.

For more complete lessons on
Ackley headspace see the book:

Chambering for Ackley Cartridges
by Fred Zeglin

ISBN# 978-0-9831598-3-4

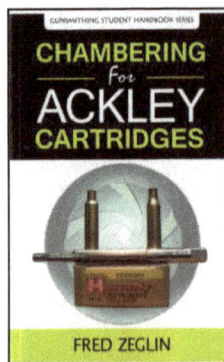

*Forster's Datum Dial, can be used to check headspace gauges or ammo for correct headspace.*

*Reloaders often set the headspace of the ammo wrong, either making it hard for the gun to lock up properly, or creating excessive headspace by bumping the shoulder back. This tool makes it easy to check ammo and prove to the client an error.*

*Note: the indicator reads .0035" this is the difference between the two gauges in the picture. Well within tolerances.*

On the next page we reprinted the PTG Ackley Improved headspace sheet. It is designed to help you understand how the headspace is measured at the junction of the neck and shoulder, rather that the SAAMI standard method.

To reiterate: this method only applies to bottle necked cases that headspace on the shoulder.

# ACKLEY IMPROVED HEADSPACE

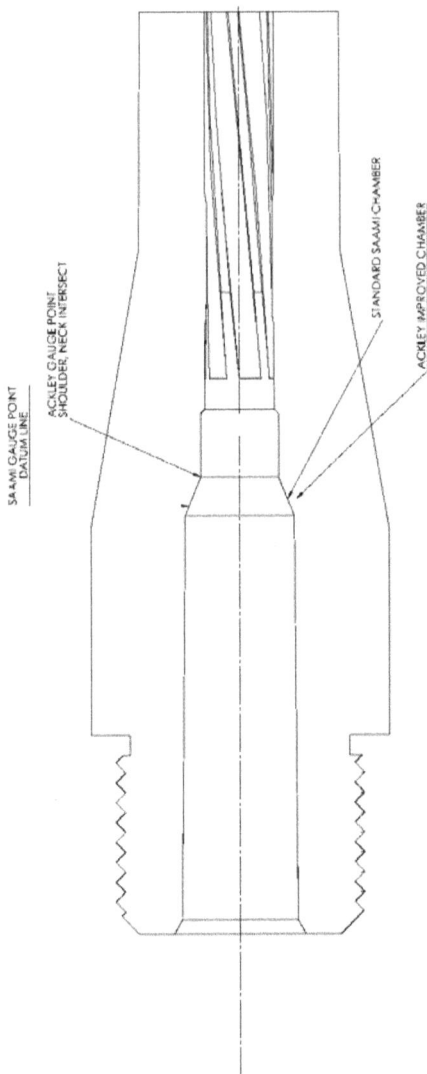

SAAMI GAUGE POINT DATUM LINE

ACKLEY GAUGE POINT SHOULDER, NECK INTERSECT

STANDARD SAAMI CHAMBER

ACKLEY IMPROVED CHAMBER

Ackley's method was simple, he used a headspace gauge .004" shorter than the SAAMI minimum chamber as a GO Gauge. The shoulder angle on the gauge was still the same as the parent chamber. Ackley used the shoulder and neck junction as his gauging point not the datum line of the SAAMI chamber. So the SAAMI GO dimension becomes the NO-GO dimension for Ackley's improved chambers, and the chamber Go minimum was .004 shorter. This shorter headspace assured that the SAAMI spec cartridges would be held tight between the breach and the junction of the neck and shoulder of the chamber during fire forming. This is called the crush fit in Mr Ackley book.

In the chart that begins on the next page the Gauge Name on the left is the most common name for the gauges. You can buy gauges marked for any cartridge in the "Family". Naturally, they are interchangeable too.

# Headspace Gauge Interchange Chart

| GAUGE NAME | USE WITH THESE CARTRIDGES |
|---|---|
| Remington BR | 17 BR, 20 BR, 22 BR, 25 BR, 6mm BR, 6.5mm BR, 270 BR, 7mm BR, 30 BR, 338 BR |
| BRX | 22 BRX, 30 BRX, 6mm BRX, 6.5 BRX |
| Dasher | 20 Dasher, 22 Dasher, 6mm Dasher, 30 Dasher, 7mm Dasher |
| PPC Gages | 22 PPC, 6mm PPC, 6.5mm PPC, 7mm PPC, 30 PPC |
| TCU | 6mm TCU, 25 TCU, 6.5 TCU, 7mm TCU |
| 22 Long Rifle (RF) | 22 Short, 22 Long, 22 Bentz, 22 Match, 17 HMII, 17 HS, 17 Aguila |
| 22 WRFM | 22 Winchester Magnum, 17 HMR |
| 22 Hornet | Hornet Based Wildcats, 17 Hornet, 22 K-Hornet |
| 221 Remington Fireball | 221 Remington Fireball, 30-221 221 Wildcats, 300 AAC, 300 TIW |
| 223 Remington | 6X45, 5.56 NATO, 17-223, 20 Practical, 223 Wylde |
| 222 Remington | 14/222, 17/222, 20/222/ 6mm/222 |
| 222 Remington Magnum | 6 X 47 Remington, 7 x 47, 17/222 Magnum |
| 22 Nosler | 6/22 Nosler 20/22 Nosler |
| 223 Winchester Super Short Magnum | 243 WSSM, 358 Indy |

| GAUGE NAME | USE WITH THESE CARTRIDGES |
|---|---|
| 22-250 | 17-250, 20-250, 6mm-250 |
| 225 Winchester | 17/225, 270/225, 6.5mm/222, 7mm/225 |
| 6mm XC | 22 XC |
| 6mm Remington | 244 Remington, 224 TTH, 22/244 |
| 240 Weatherby | 22-240 Weatherby |
| 6.17 Spitfire | 6.71 Phantom |
| 6.53 Scramjet | 6.17 Flash |
| 25-20 | 17 Ackley Bee, 17 Hebee, 218 Bee, 218 Mashburn Bee, 32-20 |
| 250 Savage | 6mm/250, 6.5mm/250, 270 Savage, 7mm/250 |
| 6.5 x 47 Lapua | 6x47 Lapua, 20x47 Lapua, 22x47 Lapua, 30x47 Lapua |
| 6.5 x 47 Lapua Ackley Improved | 6mm Long Dasher |
| 6.5 Grendel | 6mm Grendel, 6mm BPC, 6.5mm BPC, 264 LBC-AR |
| 6.5 Creedmoor | 22 Creedmoor, 6mm Creedmoor, 25 Creedmoor, 7mm Creedmoor, 30 Creedmoor, 8.6 Creedmoor |
| 26 Nosler | 28 Nosler (all other Nosler calibers have specific gauges) |
| 6.8 SPC | 6.8 SPC II, 6mm SPC II |
| 7 X 57 | 257 Roberts, 6.5-257 Roberts, 270X57, 7mm Mauser, 9.3x57 Mauser |

| GAUGE NAME | USE WITH THESE CARTRIDGES |
|---|---|
| 280 Remington | 7mm Express |
| 284 Winchester | 22/284, 6/284, 25/284, 6.5/284, 270/284, 30/284, 338/284, 35/284, 6.5/284 Norma, 6.5/284 Lapua, 284 Shehane |
| 7.21 Firehawk | 6.71 Blackbird |
| 30-30 WCF | 19 Zipper, 219 Zipper, 219 Zipper Imp., 219 Donaldson Wasp, 22/30-30, 25-35 WCF, 7-30 Waters, 7mm Int. Rimmed, 30-30 Based Wildcats, 30 Herrett, 303 Savage, 307 Win., 32-40 WCF, 32 Win. Spl., 356 Win., 357 Herrett, 375 Win., 38-55 WCF, 444 Marlin |
| 30 IHMSA | 6mm IHMSA, 7mm IHMSA |
| 30 Remington | 32 Remington |
| 300 Savage | 270/300 Savage |
| 30-40 Krag | 303 British, Krag wildcats, 40-70 Straight, 35 Winchester |
| 308 Winchester | 7.62x51 NATO, 22/243, 243 Win., 260 Rem., 7/08, 338-08, 338 Federal, 358 Win., 25 Souper, 6.5 Panther |
| 30-06 | 22/06, 6mm/06, 25/06, 6.5/06, 270 Win., 8mm/06, 338/06, 35 Whelen, 375-06, 375 Whelen, 7mm/06 |
| 30 Gibbs | 22 SS, 240 Gibbs, 25 Gibbs, 6.5 Gibbs, 270 Gibbs, 33 Gibbs, 35 Gibbs, 7mm Gibbs |

| GAUGE NAME | USE WITH THESE CARTRIDGES |
|---|---|
| 300 H&H | See Belted Magnum |
| 7.62 Patriot | 8.59 Galaxy, 7.21 Tomahawk |
| 300 WSM | 270 WSM, 6.5/300 WSM, 6.5 Leopard, 325 WSM<br>**(7mm WSM has specific gauge)** |
| 300 RSAUM (SAUM) | 6.5/300 RSAUM, 270 RSAUM, 7mm RSAUM and 338 RSAUM |
| 300 (RUM) Remington Ultra Mag | 270 Ultra Mag, 7mm Ultra Mag, 375 Ultra Mag, 338 Edge, UltraCat (wildcats)<br>(DO NOT USE with .338 Ultra Mag) |
| 7.82 Warbird | 8.59 Titan, 10.75 Meteor, 7.62 Firebird |
| 32 H&R Magnum | 32 S&W Long, 32 Colt's, 32 Short Colt, 32 Colt Long |
| 8mm Mauser | 8x57 |
| 348 Winchester (WCF) | 45-70, 450 Alaskan, 50 Alaskan |
| 416 Rigby | 450 Rigby |
| 9mm Luger | 9x19, 9mm NATO, 9mm Parabelum, 9mm |
| 357 Magnum | 22 Remington Jet, 22/256, 256 Winchester Magnum, 357 Maximum, 38 Special, 38 S&W |
| 358 Winchester | 308, 7mm/08, 243 Winchester |
| 35 Whelen | 30-06, 270, 338-06 |

| GAUGE NAME | USE WITH THESE CARTRIDGES |
|---|---|
| 375 Winchester | 30-30, 38-55, 32 Win. |
| 378 Weatherby | 6.5/378 Wby, 30/378 Wby., 338/378 Wby., .416 Wby., 460 Wby., 378 or 460 Based Wildcats |
| 38 Super | 38 Super, 38 Super Match, 38 Super Nonte |
| 40-65 | 45-70, 348 Win. |
| 44-40 WCF | 38-40 WCF |
| 44 Remington Magnum | 357/44 Bain-Davis, 44 Special, 44 S&W, 44 S&W Russian, 45 S&W Schofield, 445 Super Mag., 45 Colt, 45 Long Colt, 454 Casull, 460 S&W |
| 45-70 Government | 6.5/348, 7/348, 30/348, 33 Win., 348 Win., 40-65 WCF, 45 Basic (45-120 3 1/4"), 40-82, 45-90, 45-110, 45-120, 450 Alaskan, 50-70, 50-90, 50 Alaskan, 50-110, 50-140 |
| 45 Colt | 454 Casull, 45 Long Colt, 44 Magnum, 44 Special, 357/44 Bain-Davis |
| 460 Weatherby | 378 Weatherby, 30-378, 338-378, 416 Wby. |

| GAUGE NAME | USE WITH THESE CARTRIDGES |
|---|---|
| Standard Belted Magnum<br><br>(H&H) | .535" Base Belted Magnum Calibers:<br>244 H&H, 250 Ackley Mag., 257 Wby, 264 Win, 6.5 Rem. Mag, 270 Wby,<br>275 H&H, 7mm Rem. Mag,<br>7mm/300 Winchester, 7mm/300 Practical, 7mm Wby, 7x61 S&H,<br>7mm STW, 300 H&H, 300 Win. Mag,<br>30-338, 300 Wby, 308 Norma Mag, 8mm Rem. Mag, 338 Win. Mag,<br>340 Wby, 350 Rem. Mag,<br>358 Norma Mag, 358 STA, 375 H&H, 375 Super Mashburn, 416 Taylor,<br>416 Rem. Mag, 458 Win. Mag, 458 Lott. |

If your chosen cartridge is not listed, it is very likely that it has a specific (unique) gauge that cannot be substituted. I.E. there is no alternate. Call the reamer maker for help.

Books like "Cartridges of the World" by Frank Barnes or "Cartridge Comparison Guide" by Andrew Chamberlain can be very useful in understanding cartridge families. They also include a wealth of information that will aid you in becoming knowledgeable about cartridge selection and ballistics.

Add to those books a selection of reloading manuals and you will be ready to work out many problems and make informed decisions that benefit you and the projects you build, whether personal of professional.

# CROWNING &
# MUZZLE TOOLS

There are numerous ways to crown a barrel, whether rifle, shotgun or pistol. Many gunsmiths simply do this work in the lathe with a tool ground to create the shape of crown the end user desires.

Reamer makers offer several tools designed to make this work faster and more profitable, not to mention very uniform. There are hand tools such as those that Brownells™ offers, pictured here.

These tools are offered in kits or separately. 90 degree facing, 45 degree chamfer tools and 11 (79) degree crowning tools. They can all be used by hand if you do not have power tools, or can be used in a lathe, drill press, or variable hand drill. They work best a slow RPMs with lots of oil.

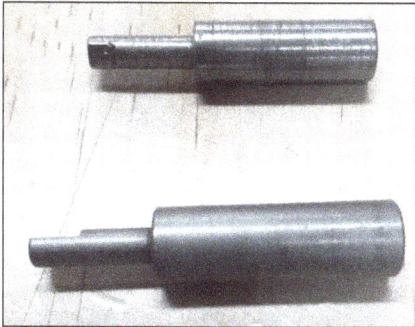

*Left are two steel pilots as offered with the muzzle facing tools above. Note first the flats for set screws, align the flat with the set screw when preparing to use.*

*The top bushing was abused, you can see the scratches and damage caused most likely by chips left on the tool or in the bore of the barrel during the cutting process. Use cutting oils and clean your pilot and bore.*

*Manson Tools offers a hand crowning tool system that does a very nice job and leaves a nice finished crown.*

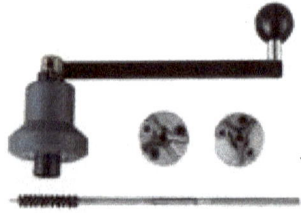

There are many crowning tools designed for use in a lathe. Offered for shotgun and rifle crowns primarily, some of them will work on handguns depending on the configuration of the barrel. You will have to pay attention and make sure there is clearance if you have a rib, or sight to deal with.

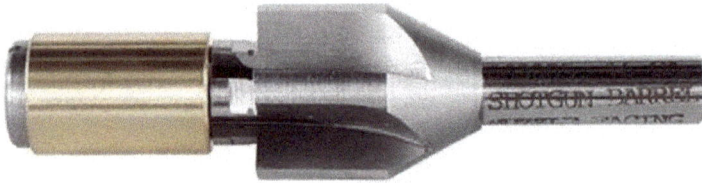

*Shotgun 90 degree facing/crown tool.*

This is form cutting, crowing tool that cuts steps and angles all in one pass. The pilot bushing is not on the tool in picture. Normally these tools will do more than one caliber by changing the pilot diameter to match the barrel.

Just like chamber reamers the pilot should be a nice slip fit to the bore with no bind or tight fit as this can damage the pilot, the tool or the barrel.

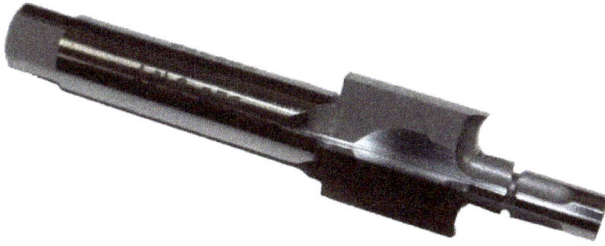

Above is a round crown tool. This design uses interchangeable Pilot bushings, although you need several sizes of cutters if you want a wide range of calibers. Otherwise your crown will look funny. Don't be a crown clown.

## Annular Cutters for Muzzle Reduction

Annular cutters are a repurposed tool. These are actually hole saws. It so happens that some of them have internal diameters that are appropriate if not perfect for muzzle diameters, when installing flash hiders, muzzle breaks or suppressors.

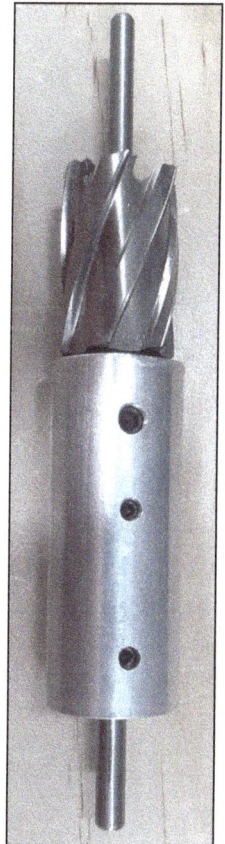

At right an annular cutter as adapted for use as a muzzle diameter tool. The holder below the cutter is used to hold the cutter and pilot aligned. This keeps the tool centered on the bore so that when you thread the muzzle it will be aligned to the bore.

Annular cutters are large diameter, so if you run them too fast they burn up quickly. Keep the RPMs low, under 250, about 100 is probably ideal.

Use lots of cutting oil on the solid pilot and on the cutter. If the pilot is too tight for your bore **make a pilot that fits.** A tight pilot in the bore will damage the pilot, and could damage the bore and/or crown.

At left, the business end of an annular cutter. You can see the pilot hole through the adapter and the six teeth that do the cutting as the muzzle.

Most of the users of these tools do not have a lathe in their shop. A lathe would be the preferred way to turn down the muzzle and thread for a muzzle device of any kind. If you have a lathe you probably do not need these tools.

**Thread Alignment Tool (TAT)**

Once you have the muzzle cut to the correct diameter for the thread you plan to use, a die can be used either for cleanup of work started on the lathe, or in combination with annular cutters for those who do not have a lathe.

Thread the TAT into the die you plan to use on the muzzle. The pilot matches the bore diameter you are working with.

The TAT must be deep enough in the die so that the threading action can start on the muzzle. That way as you thread down the barrel the TAT bumps against the muzzle and is pushed back out of the die. If you feel the TAT binding against the muzzle, manually back in up so the die can cut. The TAT pictured here has a screw driver slot, some version have hex key cavities.

A TAT is the best way to insure the die is aligned with the bore of the barrel.

Working by hand without a TAT there is no way to know if your threads are aligned to the bore. Misaligned threads could mean a damaged muzzle device, or worse.

# Appendix I  Reamer, Removable Pilot Bushings

| 17 Caliber Pilot Diameters | | | | Standard pilots for bore | | Standard Bore |
|---|---|---|---|---|---|---|
| Undersized | | .1655 | .166 | .1665 | .167 | .1675 | .168 |
| Oversized | | | .1685 | .169 | | | |

| 22 Caliber Pilot Diameters | | | | | Standard pilots for bore | | Standard Bore | Standard Cylinder |
|---|---|---|---|---|---|---|---|---|
| Undersized Rimfire | .213 | .214 | .215 | .2155 | .216 | .2165 | .217 | .222 |
| Undersized Centerfire | | | .216 | .2165 | .217 | .2175 | .218/.219 | .224 |
| Oversized Centerfire | | .2185 | .219 | .2195 | | | | |

| 6mm/243 Caliber Pilot Diameters | | | | Standard pilots for bore | | Standard Bore |
|---|---|---|---|---|---|---|
| Undersized | | .2345 | .235 | .2355 | .236 | .2365 | .237 |
| Oversized | | | .237 | .2375 | | | |

| 25/257 Caliber Pilot Diameters | | | | Standard pilots for bore | | Standard Bore |
|---|---|---|---|---|---|---|
| Undersized | | .2475 | .248 | .2485 | .249 | .2495 | .250 |
| Oversized | | | .2505 | .251 | | | |

| 6.5mm/264 Caliber Pilot Diameters | | | | Standard pilots for bore | | Standard Bore |
|---|---|---|---|---|---|---|
| Undersized | | .2535 | .254 | .2545 | .255 | .2555 | .256 |
| Oversized | | | .2565 | .257 | | | |

| 6.8mm/270 Caliber Pilot Diameters | | | | Standard pilots for bore | | Standard Bore |
|---|---|---|---|---|---|---|
| Undersized | | .2675 | .268 | .2685 | .269 | .2695 | .270 |
| Oversized | | .270 | .2705 | .271 | | | |

| 7mm/284 Caliber Pilot Diameters | | | | Standard pilots for bore | | Standard Bore |
|---|---|---|---|---|---|---|
| Undersized | .274 | .2745 | .275 | .2755 | .276 | .2765 | .277 |
| Oversized | | | .2765 | .277 | | | |

| 30/308/7.62mm Caliber Pilot Diameters | | | | Standard pilots for bore | | Standard Bore |
|---|---|---|---|---|---|---|
| Undersized | .297 | .2975 | .298 | .2985 | .299 | .2995 | .300 |
| Oversized | .3005 | .301 | .3015 | .302 | | | |

| 32/311 Caliber Pilot Diameters (pistol) | | | | Standard pilots for bore | | Standard Bore | Standard Cylinder |
|---|---|---|---|---|---|---|---|
| Undersized | | .300 | .301 | .3015 | .302 | .3025 | .303 | .313 |
| Oversized | | | .3035 | .304 | | | | |

| 8mm/32 Caliber Pilot Diameters | | | | Standard pilots for bore | | Standard Bore |
|---|---|---|---|---|---|---|
| Undersized | .310 | .311 | .312 | .313 | .314 | .3145 | .315 |
| Oversized | | | .3155 | .316 | | | |

| 338/340/8.6mm Caliber Pilot Diameters | | | | | Standard pilots for bore | | Standard Bore |
|---|---|---|---|---|---|---|---|
| Undersized | | .327 | .328 | .3285 | .329 | .3295 | .330 |
| Oversized | | | .3305 | .331 | | | |

| 9mm Caliber Pilot Diameters (pistol) | | | | | Standard pilots for bore | | Standard Bore | Standard Cylinder |
|---|---|---|---|---|---|---|---|---|
| Undersized | .3425 | .343 | .344 | .3445 | .345 | .3455 | .346 | .356/.355 |
| Oversized | | | .3475 | .348 | | | | |

| 357/38 Caliber Pilot Diameters (pistol) | | | | | Standard pilots for bore | | Standard Bore | Standard Cylinder |
|---|---|---|---|---|---|---|---|---|
| Undersized | | .3435 | .344 | .3445 | .345 | .3455 | .346 | .357 |
| Oversized | | | .3505 | .351 | | | | |

| 358 Caliber Pilot Diameters | | | | | Standard pilots for bore | | Standard Bore |
|---|---|---|---|---|---|---|---|
| Undersized | .347 | .3475 | .348 | .3485 | .349 | .3495 | 350 |
| Oversized | | | .3505 | .351 | | | |

| 9.3mm/36 Caliber Pilot Diameters | | | | | Standard pilots for bore | | Standard Bore |
|---|---|---|---|---|---|---|---|
| Undersized | | | .3515 | .352 | .3525 | .353 | .3535 |
| Oversized | | | .354 | .3545 | | | |

| 375 Caliber Pilot Diameters | | | | | Standard pilots for bore | | Standard Bore |
|---|---|---|---|---|---|---|---|
| Undersized | .362 | .3625 | .363 | .3635 | .364 | .3645 | .365 |
| Oversized | .3665 | .367 | .3675 | .368 | | | |

| 10mm/40 Caliber Pilot Diameters (pistol) | | | | | Standard pilots for bore | | Standard Bore | Standard Cylinder |
|---|---|---|---|---|---|---|---|---|
| Undersized | . | | .388 | .3885 | 389 | .3895 | .390 | .400 |
| Oversized | .391 | .392 | .3925 | | | | | |

| 408 Caliber Pilot Diameters | | | | | Standard pilots for bore | | Standard Bore |
|---|---|---|---|---|---|---|---|
| Undersized | .397 | .3975 | .398 | .3985 | .399 | .3995 | .400 |
| Oversized | | | .4005 | .401 | | | |

| 41 Caliber Pilot Diameters (pistol) | | | | | Standard pilots for bore | | Standard Bore | Standard Cylinder |
|---|---|---|---|---|---|---|---|---|
| Undersized | .396 | .3965 | .397 | .3975 | .398 | .3985 | .399 | .410 |
| Oversized | | .399 | .3995 | .400 | | | | |

| 405/411/412 Caliber Pilot Diameters | | | | | Standard pilots for bore | | Standard Bore |
|---|---|---|---|---|---|---|---|
| Undersized | .409 | .4095 | .410 | .4105 | .411 | .4115 | 412 |
| Oversized | | .4125 | .413 | .4135 | | | |

| 416 Caliber Pilot Diameters | | | | | Standard pilots for bore | | Standard Bore |
|---|---|---|---|---|---|---|---|
| Undersized | .405 | .4055 | .406 | .4065 | .407 | .4075 | .408 |
| Oversized | | | .4085 | .409 | .4095 | | |

| 44 Caliber Pilot Diameters (pistol) | | | | Standard pilots for bore | | Standard Bore | Standard Cylinder |
|---|---|---|---|---|---|---|---|
| Undersized | | .4145 | .415 | .4155 | ..416 | .4165 | .417 | .430 |
| Oversized | .417 | .4175 | .418 | .4185 | | | | |
| MicroGroove | .421 | .4215 | .422 | .4225 | .423 | .4235 | .424 | |

| 45 Caliber Pilot Diameters (pistol) | | | | Standard pilots for bore | | Standard Bore | Standard Cylinder |
|---|---|---|---|---|---|---|---|
| Undersized | | | .440 | .4405 | .441 | .4415 | .442 | .451 |
| Oversized | | .4425 | .443 | .4435 | | | | |

| 458 Caliber Pilot Diameters | | | | Standard pilots for bore | | Standard Bore |
|---|---|---|---|---|---|---|
| Undersized | .447 | .4475 | .448 | .4485 | .449 | .4495 | .450 |
| Oversized | .450 | .4505 | .451 | .4515 | | | |

| 475 Caliber Pilot Diameters | | | | Standard pilots for bore | | Standard Bore | Standard Cylinder |
|---|---|---|---|---|---|---|---|
| Undersized | | .456 | .45645 | .457 | .4575 | .458 | .458 | .476 |
| Oversized | .4585 | .459 | .4595 | .460 | | | | |

| 500 Caliber Pilot Diameters (pistol) | | | | Standard pilots for bore | | Standard Bore | Standard Cylinder |
|---|---|---|---|---|---|---|---|
| Undersized | .483 | .484 | .485 | .486 | .487 | .4875 | .488 | 500 |
| Oversized | .4885 | .489 | .490 | | | | | |

| 50 Caliber Pilot Diameters | | | | Standard pilots for bore | | Standard Bore |
|---|---|---|---|---|---|---|
| Undersized | .4965 | .497 | .4975 | .498 | .4985 | .499 | .500 |
| Oversized | | | .5005 | .501 | | | |

| 577 Caliber (.585) Pilot Diameters | | | | Standard pilots for bore | | Standard Bore |
|---|---|---|---|---|---|---|
| Undersized | .5735 | .574 | .5745 | .575 | .5755 | .576 | .577 |
| Oversized | | .5765 | .5775 | .578 | | | |

Bushing style pilots can be ordered in any diameter you need. Some gunsmiths stock a set of six to ten bushings for each bore diameter. You could call that an investment in accuracy.

## Appendix II

The chart below shows the standard bushing specifications that most of the industry are using now. In the event that you have to make your own bushings this could save you a lot of time.

# Bushing Reference Chart

| Pilot Size | Caliber Range | O.D. Range | I.D. | OAL |
|---|---|---|---|---|
| **High Speed Steel Reamers** | | | | |
| #00 | 16-17 Cal. | .145-.190 | .125 | .499 |
| #0 | 19-21 Cal. | .190-.215 | .175 | .499 |
| #1 | 22-243 Cal. | .215-.243 | .189 | .499 |
| #2 | 25-29 Cal. | .249-.277 | .220 | .499 |
| #3 | 30-49 Cal. | .278-.499 | .252 | .499 |
| #4 | 50-62 Cal | .500-620 | .312 | .499 |
| #5 | 62-20mm | .620-1.140 | .500 | .999 |
| #6 | 30mm | 1.140+ | .625 | .999 |
| **Carbide Reamers** | | | | |
| #0 | 17-220 Cal. | .160-.219 | .125 | .749 |
| #1 | 22-243 Cal. | .220-.285 | .162 | .749 |
| #2 | 243-290 Cal. | .243-.290 | .175 | .749 |
| #3 | 30-49 Cal. | .290-.499 | .225 | .749 |
| #4 | 50-62 Cal. | 500-.620 | .3125 | .999 |
| #5 | 30mm | 1.140+ | .625 | .999 |

# Afterword

As a professional educator of future gunsmiths, I can say from experience that good reference materials on gunsmithing related subjects are quite rare. Those who possess the highly specialized technical knowledge necessary to produce such references are often either unwilling to pass on their hard won "secrets", or simply too busy making a living plying their trade.

It is refreshing to see a departure from this trend, when those with the ability freely share their knowledge. In the case of this text, a highly skilled gunsmith with decades in the industry has shared his considerable insights regarding something he is intimately familiar with: chambering reamers and other gunsmithing specific cutting tools and gauges.

Specialized forming tools such as chambering reamers and forcing cone cutters are often considered to be quite mysterious, even by those who use them on a regular basis. In this Primer, Fred Zeglin has put together a concise but easily understandable text that should prove invaluable to those who seek to understand a bit more about these tools.

This was accomplished with none of the usual dogma that often accompanies such discussion. Topics such as free-bore, pilot diameter, and preventing tool chatter are presented in a very basic, matter-of-fact manner that will be useful to gunsmiths ranging from inexperienced students to seasoned professionals.

**Mark Dye**
Director of Gunsmithing Program
Montgomery Community College

# ABOUT FRED ZEGLIN...

Fred Zeglin, has been building custom rifles for over 35 years and specialized in wildcat designs for his clients. He has taught NRA Gunsmithing courses in Wildcat Cartridge Design at Murray State College in Oklahoma and Trinidad State Junior College in Colorado. Fred also worked with AGI to create a lessons on DVD called "Taming Wildcats" and "Reloading A to Z".

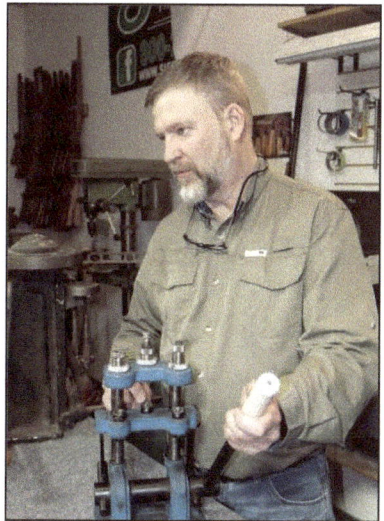

Fred has written articles for Precision Shooting Magazine, Guns and Ammo, and many others. He has hosted an award winning podcast about gunsmithing at:
http://www.stitcher.com/podcast/gunsmithing-radio
Fred also writes a gunsmithing blog that can be found at:
https://gunsmithtalk.wordpress.com

Fred has published other books including, "Hawk Cartridges Manual", "Wildcat Cartridges, Reloader's Handbook of Wildcat Cartridge Design." and "P.O. Ackley, America's Gunsmith" All available on Amazon.

This book is part of a series of gunsmith manuals that Fred is compiling. When you teach a technical subject like gunsmithing to others, you quickly learn that you have a "Curse of Knowledge". That means you don't remember how little you knew starting out and it's important to make sure your students receive that basic information along with the more advanced concepts.

Titles in the series include: Understanding Headspace, Chambering for Ackley Cartridges and Chambering Rifle Barrels for Accuracy. With more to follow in the: "Gunsmithing Student Handbook Series".

**Gunsmithing STUDENT HANDBOOK Series**

The Primer you are holding is unusual in that we are not trying to teach gunsmithing in this book. We are trying to help gunsmiths and machinists with all levels of knowledge to understand the tools discussed here.

Everyone who participated in the assembly of this book will tell you they answer these questions on a daily basis. Which may make this the world's largest FAQ page…

This primer does a great job of explaining tools in detail. When you know how and why these tools work you are a better gunsmith. Such knowledge will make you more efficient with your time and the quality of your workmanship will improve.

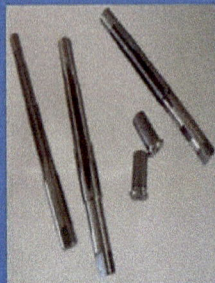

www.ingramcontent.com/pod-product-compliance
Lightning Source LLC
Chambersburg PA
CBHW051432270326
41934CB00018B/3479